MW00474043

"Richard Baxter was a skilled
this book are some of his writin,
theologian and lifelong student of Baxter. Michael Lundy is a clinical
psychiatrist who has modernized the texts of Baxter. The result is an
unusually instructive book of practical wisdom that will be a great help
to pastors and others who are called to give counsel to the downcast."

**Paul Helm,** Professor of the History and Philosophy of Religion
Emeritus, King's College, London; author, *The Providence of God*

"Here you will find two treasures for the price of one: consultations with
a practicing psychiatrist (Michael Lundy—who, by definition, is a 'healer
of the soul') and a distinguished theologian (J. I. Packer—who especially
loves authors whose theology engages what used to be called 'the cure of
souls'). But, in fact, it turns out to be three treasures for the price of one,
as a doctor of medicine and a doctor of philosophy together highlight the
wisdom of the remarkable pastor-theologian Richard Baxter. *Depression,
Anxiety, and the Christian Life* is simultaneously a manual for pastors and
counselors, a resource for study groups, and a thesaurus of wise spiritual
counsel for those who struggle and for those who care about them. A few
consultations with the soul-physician group of Packer, Lundy, and Baxter
will be medicine for your soul!"

**Sinclair B. Ferguson,** Chancellor's Professor of Systematic Theology,
Reformed Theological Seminary; Teaching Fellow, Ligonier
Ministries

"A threefold cord is not quickly broken. In this book, J. I. Packer and
Michael Lundy team up with the great Puritan Richard Baxter, who was
truly a physician of souls, to offer Christians much-needed help on the
thorny spiritual realities of depression and anxiety. Few, if any, Christians
are unfamiliar with the pain of anxiety and depression. Few, if any, will
fail to be immensely helped by the guidance offered in these pages."

**Mark Jones,** Teaching Elder, Faith Vancouver Presbyterian Church,
Vancouver, British Columbia

# DEPRESSION, ANXIETY, AND THE CHRISTIAN LIFE

# DEPRESSION, ANXIETY, AND THE CHRISTIAN LIFE

*Practical Wisdom from Richard Baxter*

Revised, Updated, and Annotated by
Michael S. Lundy, MD

Introduction by J. I. Packer

WHEATON, ILLINOIS

---

**Library of Congress Cataloging-in-Publication Data**

Names: Baxter, Richard, 1615–1691, author. | Lundy, Michael S., 1953– annotator.
Title: Depression, anxiety, and the Christian life: practical wisdom from Richard Baxter / annotated by Michael S. Lundy, MD; introduction by J. I. Packer.
Description: Wheaton: Crossway, 2018. | Includes bibliographical references and index.
Identifiers: LCCN 2017057944 (print) | LCCN 2018021481 (ebook) | ISBN 9781433542077 (pdf) | ISBN 9781433542084 (mobi) | ISBN 9781433542091 (epub) | ISBN 9781433542060 (tp)
Subjects: LCSH: Anxiety—Religious aspects—Christianity. | Depression, Mental—Religious aspects—Christianity. | Depressed persons—Religious life.
Classification: LCC BV4908.5 (ebook) | LCC BV4908.5 .B39 2018 (print) | DDC 248.8/6—dc23
LC record available at https://lccn.loc.gov/2017057944

---

# CONTENTS

Preface by J. I. Packer ................................................ 9

**PART 1   INTRODUCING RICHARD BAXTER**

1   Richard Baxter, Spiritual Physician ........................17
    *J. I. Packer*

2   Richard Baxter: Perspective and Retrospective.............35
    *Michael S. Lundy, MD*

**PART 2   BAXTER'S COUNSEL ON DEPRESSION**

3   Advice to Depressed and Anxious Christians ..............73
    *Richard Baxter*

4   The Resolution of Depression and Overwhelming Grief
    through Faith ............................................... 103
    *Richard Baxter*

Appendix: The Duty of Physicians ........................... 169
    *Richard Baxter*

General Index ................................................. 177

Scripture Index ............................................... 181

# PREFACE

The following pages are a joint effort intended as a "threefold cord," as it were.[1] James Packer, a pastor-teacher, and Michael Lundy, a physician-psychiatrist, were drawn together by a shared admiration for Richard Baxter (1615–1691), a classic Puritan writer on the Christian life, perhaps best known for his work *The Reformed Pastor*. One of Baxter's main concerns as a pastor was to relieve depression. Resonating with Baxter's concern, Lundy and Packer came to think that a mini-treatise by Baxter that, at its heart, sought to serve the depressed would, if republished in a modern edition, be a valuable resource for pastoral care of depressed persons in today's churches. Hence this book. While it will be apparent that Dr. Packer drafted the first chapter introducing Baxter, and Dr. Lundy wrote the second and edited and updated the Baxter texts in part 2, both of us endorse everything affirmed here.

## What Is Depression?

Depression is our focus, but what is that? Generalizing, we may say that the term pictures downward pressure squeezing out and draining away whatever modes of energy and eagerness were there before. For more than a century the word's

---

1. "A threefold cord is not quickly broken" (Eccles. 4:12).

chief use has been psychological. A recent dictionary defines depression as "a state of extreme dejection or morbidly excessive melancholy; a mood of hopelessness and feelings of inadequacy, often with physical symptoms such as loss of appetite, insomnia, etc."[2] Sooner or later most of us experience some form of this, maybe fleetingly as the product of trauma, strain, overwork, or something of the kind, maybe in a more long-term, habitual, deeper-rooted way, and we are told to expect that two-thirds of North Americans will at some stage need and seek treatment for depression. It is a condition that is apparently becoming increasingly common in our hustling, bustling, jostling, cacophonous culture, and seems set to continue to do so.

What happens in depression? Still generalizing, we say: fretful heaviness seizes the mind, sometimes slowing it down to a point of virtual paralysis where thought ceases, sometimes driving it into unfruitful randomness, or a fixed attitude of gloom, or an incessant harping on things felt to be incurably wrong. Depressed persons feel themselves isolated and distant from others—even their nearest and dearest—and from projects in which hitherto their hearts had been fully engaged. Conduct may become eccentric, randomness or inaction may set in, focused creativity may fade away, or sadness may become habitual. Feelings of anxiety, worthlessness, and hopelessness develop, and defensive pessimism takes over. Upset by others' cheerfulness, the depressed may seem cross-grained and combative. Some depressions are cyclical, low points in bipolar mood swings, where they may be followed by bursts of energetic overconfidence. What medication can do to modify these extremes varies from person to person.

---

2. *Canadian Oxford English Dictionary*, ed. Katherine Barber (Don Mills, ON: Oxford University Press, 1998), s.v.

C. H. Spurgeon, England's greatest nineteenth-century gospel preacher, suffered periodic bouts of depression. Causeless as they seemed, their impact was heavy; fighting them was, as he put it, like fighting mist, and he had to wait till the "shapeless, undefinable, yet all-beclouding hopelessness" lifted from his heart.[3] The "black dog" of Winston Churchill's middle years seems to have been similar.[4]

When God let Satan have his way with Job, an extreme case of traumatic shock, bewilderment, frustration, misery, and hopelessness, with biting negativity toward his know-it-all friends resulted, as we are shown. All these qualities crowded together, as it were—each with its own pain—under the umbrella of depression formed an archetypal instance of this affliction.

For a full century depression has been intensely studied from various angles, and there are many books on it, reflecting predominantly post-Christian, secular perspectives. Our own standpoint, however, is somewhat different.

## Our Standpoint

Our ideal for all Christians, ourselves included, is to live as far as possible in the outgoing love, stability, and joy—along with patience, kindness, faithfulness, and self-control[5]—that form the moral profile of Jesus Christ in his disciples. We see such living as true human flourishing, and the promotion of it as

---

3. C. H. Spurgeon, "Lecture XI: The Minister's Fainting Fits," in *Lectures to My Students*, vol. 1, *A Selection of Addresses Delivered to the Students of the Pastors' College, Metropolitan Tabernacle* (New York: Sheldon, 1975), 263.

4. For a brief read on Churchill's "black dog," see John H. Mather, "Winston Churchill and the 'Black Dog of Depression,'" review of *Churchill and the 'Black Dog' of Depression: Reassessing the Biographical Evidence of Psychological Disorder*, by Wilfred Attenborough, *The Churchill Project, Hillsdale College*, January 20, 2016, https://winstonchurchill.hillsdale.edu/winston-churchill-and-the-black-dog-of-depression-by-wilfred-attenborough/.

5. Our echo of Gal. 5:22–23 is not accidental: "But the fruit of the Spirit is love, joy, peace, patience, kindness, goodness, faithfulness, gentleness, self-control; against such things there is no law."

central to all forms of pastoral care, church worship and fellowship, personal therapy, and Christian family life. And we see depression in all its forms as a prima facie obstruction to this, in which Satan regularly has a hand (see 2 Cor. 12:7).[6] We believe that in the wisdom of God thorns in the flesh—mental and emotional thorns included—may become means of spiritual advance that would not otherwise take place. And we believe that greater wisdom in this matter than we are used to is found in the pastoral heritage of seventeenth-century Puritanism. Supreme here is the wisdom of Richard Baxter, who in his day was viewed and consulted as a top authority regarding ministry to Christians afflicted by what was then called "melancholy," but would today be labeled depression. Our hope is that by presenting what Baxter wrote in this field we may contribute to wise pastoral care in Bible-believing, gospel-centered, Christ-honoring churches at this time.

The plan of this volume, following our introductory chapters, is to reproduce two addresses by Richard Baxter, as well as a shorter essay in the appendix, and to indicate how his wisdom may be brought into the twenty-first century to become a resource for ministry today. Chapter 3, "Advice to Depressed and Anxious Christians," offers an edited and updated version of Baxter's "Directions to the Melancholy about Their Thoughts," in his *Christian Directory*. Chapter 4, "The Resolution of Depression and Overwhelming Grief through Faith," edits and updates Baxter's "The Cure of Melancholy and Overmuch Sorrow, by Faith." The appendix does the same for Baxter's "The Duty of Physicians," also in *A Christian Directory*.

For the past century and more the notion has been abroad in evangelical circles that the effect of being born again through

---

6. "So to keep me from becoming conceited because of the surpassing greatness of the revelations, a thorn was given me in the flesh, a messenger of Satan to harass me, to keep me from becoming conceited" (2 Cor. 12:7).

faith in Jesus Christ will always be a life marked by spiritual euphoria: constant cheerfulness, exuberance, confidence, and high spirits stemming from the knowledge that the God of grace, the sovereign triune Lord, is always actively on one's side. Indeed he is, and the picture drawn is an attractive and happy one—but see what it leaves out! Certainly triumphant joy in the Lord is a characteristic feature of a healthy Christian life. But Christians, like other people, live in and through bodies—bodies that from time to time malfunction, get sick, wear out, and finally die; and physical factors, with or without spiritual slippages, can at any stage bring on, among other things, depression in its various forms. Some in the past have gone so far as to diagnose depression in Christians as always a sign of unbelief or some other major sin, but this is not right.

For more than four centuries Bunyan's *Pilgrim's Progress*, one of the world's best sellers, has been reminding Christians that the normal Christian life involves not only assurances and joy but also battles: battles against sin in both one's heart and one's life; battles against temptation arising from circumstances; battles against despair, brought on by foolish missteps and failures; and battles against hopelessness, triggered by a sense of inadequacy that induces depression. All this Bunyan portrays in the characters of Mr. Fearing, Mr. Despondency, Mr. Feeble-Mind, and Mr. Ready-to-Halt. As today the truth that Christians only live by being constantly forgiven is constantly forgotten, and the truth of Satan's unending war with believers is rarely taken seriously, so the reality of depression as a recurring or abiding thorn in some Christians' flesh is often overlooked. We need help here, and in the estimate of the present writers, Richard Baxter is the man to give it.

J. I. Packer

# PART 1

# INTRODUCING RICHARD BAXTER

*Chapter 1*

# RICHARD BAXTER, SPIRITUAL PHYSICIAN

## J. I. Packer

Human nature does not change, but times and seasons do, and all humans are children of their own age to a greater extent than either they or those who look back to them, whether for praise or blame, tend to realize. This is notably true of the great Christian communicators of days past: Augustine, Luther, Bunyan, Whitefield, Wesley, Spurgeon, and their like. Rightly we hail as heroes our blood-brothers in the faith, and in so doing we fail to see them in terms of their own world. Richard Baxter is another such. While he transcended his time in many ways, he was very much a man of it, and we should begin our account of him by noting some key facts about the history and culture of which he was part.

## Puritanism

In his adult life Baxter was called a Puritan, a term of disrespect, but one he accepted, though increasingly he referred to himself as a "meer Christian," a cautious friend to all creedal churches and their adherents, while yet showing an unqualified commitment to none of them. "Puritan," however, tagged him as involved in a sometimes impatient and imprudent left-wing Reformational movement that had been making waves in England ever since Elizabeth's reign began.

It had developed in two directions, political and pastoral. The political wing clamored, unsuccessfully, for a radicalizing of the Elizabethan settlement in a number of ways. From its ranks were to come the revolutionaries who, provoked beyond endurance by Charles I's autocracy and bad faith, finally fought and executed him and set up the well-meant but short-lived Commonwealth. Pastorally oriented Puritans, on the other hand, gave themselves to preaching, teaching, and what we would call evangelism. Their goal was the conversion of all England to vital biblical and Reformed faith. To this end they produced a steady flow of catechetical, homiletical, and devotional literature. This was Baxter's own prime field of ministry; while he dabbled in political concerns, his main contribution was as one of Puritanism's most gifted writers of didactic devotional material, as we shall see.

The Puritan pastoral purpose can be focused as the fostering of a Reformed brand of Augustinian piety, starting with a regenerative conversion (faith in Christ, Godward repentance, assurance of justifying acceptance and adoption into God's family, worshipful communion with the Father and the Son, and daily obedience to God's law by the power of the Holy Spirit). Christian life as such would then take the form of love and service (good works) in family, church, and society, monitored by conscience pursuing its two concerns. Concern number one was the discerning of duty, that is, the specifics of God's biblically revealed will for each day's action. Concern number two was self-examination or self-search, the regular reviewing of one's motives and actions to make sure that one was living as a real believer and not a self-deluded "gospel hypocrite," as pew-sitting formalists were sometimes called. The Puritans viewed life as a landscape crisscrossed by many paths, of which one must always seek to discern and follow the most God-honoring, which will be the wisest and best for others and oneself. Casuistry was the Puritan name for study of the principles for making this choice each time, and conflict with the world, the flesh, and the Devil was understood to be involved in actually doing that. Baxter was an expert teacher in relation to all these concerns, and something like half of Kidderminster's two thousand adult inhabitants became Puritans under his instruction.

## The Life of Baxter

Richard Baxter lived from 1615 to 1691. Though sickly from his late teens on, he never lacked mental energy and enterprise. He experienced the Civil War as an army chaplain, the Commonwealth as an urban pastor, the Restoration as a pastor ejected, the persecution that followed as one who, after years of avoiding arrest for unauthorized preaching, finally spent two years in prison, and the 1689 Act of Toleration following the Revolution as bringing him full freedom for ministry for the last two years of his life. He was born and raised in rural Shropshire, in England's west Midlands; he was the son of a village gentleman in the seventeenth-century sense of that word, that is, a property owner, in this case on a small scale. Baxter's father, having gambled away much wealth, had become a serious Christian. One day he bought a Puritan devotional, Richard

Sibbes's *Bruised Reed and Smoking Flax* (1630),[1] from a peddler at the door; his son Richard read it, and it was this more than anything else that brought Richard Baxter to a serious Christian commitment at some point in his teens. He did brilliantly at school, but his father unwisely diverted him from university; however, having resolved on pastoral ministry as a career, he secured ordination in 1638. Following a year as a schoolmaster he became a "lecturer" (supplementary preacher, privately funded), first at Shropshire's Bridgnorth and then in the Midlands weaving town of Kidderminster, where, as chief pastor from 1647, he enjoyed his great success.

Tall and thin, alert and friendly, Baxter was a quick thinker, an easy and fluent speaker, a passionate preacher, a formidable debater, and a very rapid writer on a wide range of topics. He soon became known for his remarkable productivity; Charles I knew of him and referred to him as "scrib[b]ling Dick." He hit the ground running with his first devotional book, over eight hundred large quarto pages long, *The Saints' Everlasting Rest* (1650), which quickly became a best seller and was reprinted annually for the first ten years of its life. During his pastorate he was in constant production on many subjects, and after his ejection from the Church of England pastorate under the 1662 Act of Uniformity he saw writing as his prime God-given kingdom task; for the last three decades of his life, therefore, he labored accordingly, becoming the most voluminous English theological writer of all time. Most significant pastorally was his completion of a series already begun for discipling church people from their first adult steps toward personal faith and devotion for the entirety of their Christian lives. Archbishop Usher had at one time encouraged him to attempt this, and Baxter came to feel

---

1. For one of several recent editions, see Sibbes, *The Bruised Reed* (Edinburgh: Banner of Truth, 1998).

that it was a mandate from God. The titles in this series up to its final item were as follows:

> *The Right Method for a Settled Peace of Conscience and Spiritual Comfort* (1653)
> *A Treatise of Conversion* (1657)
> *A Call to the Unconverted to Turn and Live* (1658)
> *Directions and Persuasions to a Sound Conviction* (1658)
> *The Crucifying of the World by the Cross of Christ* (1658)
> *Christian Unity* (1659)
> *A Treatise of Self-Denial* (1660)
> *The Vain Religion of the Formal Hypocrite Detected* (1660)
> *The Mischiefs of Self-Ignorance and the Benefits of Self-Acquaintance* (1662)
> *Now or Never* (1662)
> *A Saint or a Brute* (1662)
> *The Divine Life* (1664)
> *Directions for Weak, Distempered Christians* (1669)
> *The Life of Faith* (1670)

And the family handbook that had been planned to round off the series had swelled by 1673, its publication date, to (I give the full title):

### A Christian Directory

*or*

*A Sum of Practical Theology, and Cases of Conscience.*

*Directing Christians How to Use Their Knowledge and Faith; How to Improve All Helps and Means, and to Perform All Duties; How to Overcome Temptations, and to Escape or Mortify Every Sin.*

*In Four Parts.*

I. *Christian Ethics (or Private Duties)*
II. *Christian Economics (or Family Duties)*
III. *Christian Ecclesiastics (or Church Duties)*
IV. *Christian Politics (or Duties to Our Rulers and Neighbours).*

(Let it be remembered that in the days before dust jackets whatever a writer wanted bookstore browsers to know about the contents of his book had to be put on the title page.) For range, size, and analytical coverage this work by Baxter was unique in its day, not to speak of ours; it is well over a million words long. During the years of his ejection Baxter also published two folios of systematic theology—one of them in Latin—and many smaller writings on church questions. His pen was never idle.

In 1662 he married Margaret Charlton, a dispossessed young gentlewoman, bright and highly strung, who after having her home destroyed in the Civil War came to assurance under Baxter's ministry. She was twenty-one years younger than Baxter, scarcely more than half his age, and they were both difficult people by ordinary standards, but it was a love match and their marriage was a happy one, something indeed of a model, as appears from the touching breviate (short account) of her life that Baxter wrote within weeks of Margaret's death in 1681.[2] Their life together was lived in and round London, where Baxter continued to live until his own death ten years later.

It was William Haller who, in 1938, first characterized Puritan pastors as physicians of the soul.[3] The phrase fits, particularly in Baxter's case. When he began his Kidderminster ministry, the town lacked a doctor, and he acted as one till he could recruit a qualified man to move there. He had evidently gained a good deal of medical knowledge from living with his own sickliness, and his sense of responsibility would have matched what he wrote in the *Directory* about "The Duty of Physicians."[4] But

2. Richard Baxter, *A Breviate of the Life of Margaret, the Daughter of Francis Charlton, of Apply in Shropshire, Esq., and Wife of Richard Baxter*. One edition of the breviate is J. I. Packer, *A Grief Sanctified: Through Sorrow to Eternal Hope* (Wheaton, IL: Crossway, 2002).
3. William Haller, *The Rise of Puritanism* (New York: Columbia University Press, 1938), chap. 1.
4. See Michael Lundy's updated version of "The Duty of Physicians" in the appendix, p. 169.

he would always have insisted that his job as a pastor required him to keep telling his people that their first task, like his, was to care for their souls, center their lives on God and the realities of eternity, seek the fullness of conversion, and aim at thorough discipleship to Christ according to the Scriptures. The pastor's God-given role as a guide in this should be seen as twofold: as a teacher and mentor in revealed truth through biblical instruction and systematic catechizing, and as spiritual health expert, able to diagnose and prescribe for spiritual well-being as need arose. By spiritual disorder Puritans meant any condition that sin in any form was shaping, while they equated spiritual health with love, service, communion with Christ, and a walk with God—in one word, *holiness*. It can fairly be said of his ministry from start to finish that Baxter was expressing in one way or another this sense of ministerial vocation, much of which he verbalized very vividly for himself and his colleagues in his 1655 classic, *The Reformed Pastor*.

## Baxter's Ground Plan for Discipling

A fuller view of the first half of *A Christian Directory* is in order here. Baxter's gift for topical analysis serves him well as he goes through all that he sees to be involved in the proper conduct of one's personal spiritual life. This overview has masterpiece quality and authority; it is fundamental and constitutes the frame within which spiritual depression is to be discerned and treated.

Following the evangelistic and catechetical material with which the *Directory* opens (for Baxter is clearly thinking of the whole work on the model of a catechism course), Baxter sets out seventeen "Grand Directions" for a "Life of Faith and Holiness: Containing the Essentials of Godliness and Christianity."[5] Abbreviated, the list looks like this:

---

5. Richard Baxter, *A Christian Directory*, pt. 1, *Christian Ethics*, chap. 3 (title).

1. Understand the nature, ground, reason, and order of faith and godliness.
2. How to live by faith in Christ.
3. How to believe in the Holy Ghost and live by his grace.
4. For a true, orderly, and practical knowledge of God.
5. Of self-resignation to God as our owner.
6. Of subjection to God as our sovereign King.
7. To learn of Christ as our teacher. The imitation of Christ.
8. To obey Christ our physician or Savior in his repairing, healing work.
9. Of Christian warfare under Christ.
10. How to work as servants of Christ our Lord.
11. To love God as our Father and felicity and end.
12. Absolutely to trust God with soul and body, and all.
13. That the temperament of our religion may be a delight in God and holiness.
14. Of thankfulness to God, our grand benefactor.
15. For glorifying God.
16. For heavenly mindedness.
17. For self-denial.

After these general "Grand Directions" come specific instructions to counter "the great sins most directly contrary to godliness":[6] unbelief, hardness of heart, hypocrisy, man-pleasing, and sensuality, plus guidance for governing one's thoughts and one's tongue, one's passions and senses, and for practicing some further forms of self-control. The work is then rounded off with detailed discussion of serving God at home and in church.

The relevance of this material for us is that it shows the quality of life to which Baxter, like other Puritans, sought to

---

6. Baxter, *Christian Ethics*, chap. 4 (title).

lead those whom he pastored, persons in depression along with the rest. Current culture sees depressives as healed when they can once more function well in society, but Puritans saw all humans as sin-sick and not in good inner health till they had learned to know Christ and to live in the manner sketched out above. Puritan counsel about depression, and about salvation, therefore, melded into one. (A fine example of this is Baxter's *The Right Method for a Settled Peace of Conscience and Spiritual Comfort*, noted above, p. 21.)

Three basic perspectives pervade all of Baxter's practical writings, each a guideline toward spiritual well-being as he understood it.

The first is the *primacy of the intellect*. All truth, so he says repeatedly, enters the soul via understanding. All motivation begins in the mind as one contemplates the realities and possibilities that draw forth affection and desire; all fellowship with Christ the Mediator also begins in the mind, with knowledge of his undying love and present risen life; all obedience begins in the mind, with recognition of revelation concerning his purpose and will. Calls to consider—to think, that is, and so get God's truth clear first in one's head and then in one's heart—are accordingly basic to Baxter's instruction. The heavily didactic, intellectually demanding quality that this imparts to his writings is, from his point of view, a necessity. It is the mind that must grasp and lead.

The second perspective is *the unity of human life before the Lord*. God made us to fulfill simultaneously two great commandments: to love God himself in his triune being, which part 1 of the *Directory* teaches us to do, and to love our neighbor as we love ourselves, which parts 2–4, on role responsibilities in the home, the church, and the community, lead us into. Note, by the way, that neighbor love, which after all is a form of charity, must begin at home; this is the biblical and Reformational emphasis. The family is mankind's primary society, and those who do not learn to love and serve their neighbors in the home—spouse, children, servants—remain hypocrites and failed disciples, however hard they may labor to serve others in the church and beyond. First things first!

The third perspective is *the centrality of eternity*. Heaven and hell are realities, and the greatness of the human soul consists partly, at least, in the fact that we will never cease to be, but must inhabit one or the other of these destinations forever. The purpose of life is to find out and follow the road to heaven, through conversion and sanctification in faith, hope, and love. In begging his hearers and readers to take eternity seriously, to think of it often, and so to run as to obtain heaven's glory, Baxter surely spoke a word that today's Christians, materially minded and this-worldly to a fault, badly need to hear. The sprawling, soaring devotional best seller mentioned above, which shot Baxter to prominence in 1650 and has been linked with his name ever since, *The Saints' Everlasting Rest*, hammers away at this theme with great emphasis, and his evangelistic and pastoral writing thereafter never lost sight of it.

## Counselor to Christians in Depression

For Puritans as a body, the good life was the godly life, and the godly life was a product of thought: thought about the framework of obligations (duties) that God has established in his Word, thought about the blood-bought forgiveness and acceptance by which Christians live, thought about God's gracious promises, thought about means to ends, and thought about the glory of God as the true goal of all created life. Puritan instruction in behavior and relationships was thus first and foremost a matter of teaching people to *think* (or, to use their regular word for this, to *consider*): to reflect, that is, on how to serve and please God in response to the truth and grace he has made known in creation, and in and through Christ. Here, however, as the Puritans clearly saw, problems arose. They knew, of course, as did and does just about everyone in the Western world, that each human being is a psychophysical unit, in which the body and the mind, though distinct, are currently inseparable, and either may make its mark functionally on the other, for better and for worse. One problem here, whereby physical factors led to a measure of mental unbalance, was what the Puritans labeled melancholy. Differently diagnosed, it remains with us today.

The word *melancholy*, which nowadays is a simple synonym for sadness, was in the seventeenth century a technical medical term. It comes from two Greek words meaning "black bile." The theory was that the human body contained four "humors" in different proportions: namely, blood, phlegm, yellow bile, and black bile. One of these, by predominating, determines each person's temperament (another technical term in those days)—that is, one's behavioral and dispositional quality. A person could be sanguine (abounding in blood: hopeful, enterprising, and liable to overdo things), or phlegmatic (cool, detached, lethargic, perhaps chillingly so), or choleric (impetuous, aggressive, sometimes explosively so), or melancholic (gloomy, pessimistic, apt to run scared and to suffer from despairing, destructive fantasies).[7] Baxter's observant, analytical mind, which fitted him to function for a time as Kidderminster's amateur physician, equipped him to focus and describe melancholy with

---

7. Baxter's adherence to this view appears when he writes that Satan can "much easier tempt a choleric person to anger, than another, and a phlegmatic, fleshly person to sloth, and a sanguine or hot-tempered person to lust, and wantonness; so also a melancholy person to thoughts of blasphemy, infidelity, and despair" (Baxter, *Christian Ethics*, chap. 6, "Directions for the Government of the Thoughts," title 5, "Directions to the Melancholy about Their Thoughts," no. 26).

precision on the basis of firsthand observational and pastoral interaction. His description can be summarized as follows:

Melancholy, as Baxter perceived it, was a psychophysical reality, a "diseased craziness . . . of the imagination"[8] that might be caused by the body being out of sorts ("sorrows that come from your spleen"),[9] or by overload or overstrain on the mind, or perhaps both together. Its symptoms were at many points recognizable as distortions of Puritan ideas and ideals that pervaded the culture. They included fantastic fears: hell-centered, running riot in head and heart; also, delusive impressions of hearing voices, seeing bright lights, feeling touches, and of being urged to blaspheme and commit suicide. Bad dreams were frequent. Melancholics characteristically could not control their thoughts; they were unable to stop despairing about everything, or to begin a discipline of thanksgiving and rejoicing in Christ, or to concentrate on anything but their own hopelessness and felt certainty of damnation. They would cultivate solitariness and idleness; they would spend hours doing nothing. They would insist that others did not understand them, and that they were not sick but only realistic about themselves, and they would prove perversely obstinate in the matter of taking medication.

The treatment that Baxter as a pastor recommended boiled down to never letting melancholics lose sight of the redeeming love of God, the free offer of life in Christ, and the greatness of grace at every point in the gospel; not attempting to practice the "secret duty" of meditation and prayer on one's own, but praying aloud in company; cultivating cheerful Christian community ("there is no mirth like the mirth of believers");[10] avoiding idleness; and making good use of a skilled physician,

---

8. Baxter, "Directions to the Melancholy," introductory par.

9. Richard Baxter, *The Right Method for a Settled Peace of Conscience and Spiritual Comfort* (1653), direct. 2, no. 2.

10. Baxter, *Right Method for a Settled Peace*, direct. 2, no. 3.

a discerning pastor, and other faithful Christian mentors and friends, for support, guidance, and hopefully a cure.

## Toward an Assessment

The measure of our appreciation of Baxter's ministry to depressed Christians will surely be the extent to which we go with his view of man, sin, and grace. There is no disputing that Puritan theology was generically Reformed, and Reformed theology was (and is) generically Augustinian, and Augustine's theology was generically Pauline and Johannine, on the basis of a view of Scripture as authoritative divine truth, unchanged and unchanging. Both Paul and John insist on the radical perversity of the fallen human heart, and the equally radical quality of the inward change that the Holy Spirit effects when he brings a person to saving faith in the Lord Jesus Christ. Tuning in to Ezekiel's imagery of the new heart and the new spirit (Ezek. 36:26),[11] Paul speaks of this change as a new creation (2 Cor. 5:17),[12] and John pictures it, as did Jesus himself, as a new birth (1 John 2:29–3:9;[13] see also John 3:3–12).[14] Puritan pastors as a body, like Baxter, saw everyone

---

11. "And I will give you a new heart, and a new spirit I will put within you. And I will remove the heart of stone from your flesh and give you a heart of flesh" (Ezek. 36:26).

12. "Therefore, if anyone is in Christ, he is a new creation. The old has passed away; behold, the new has come" (2 Cor. 5:17).

13. "If you know that he is righteous, you may be sure that everyone who practices righteousness has been born of him.

"See what kind of love the Father has given to us, that we should be called children of God; and so we are. The reason why the world does not know us is that it did not know him. Beloved, we are God's children now, and what we will be has not yet appeared; but we know that when he appears we shall be like him, because we shall see him as he is. And everyone who thus hopes in him purifies himself as he is pure.

"Everyone who makes a practice of sinning also practices lawlessness; sin is lawlessness. You know that he appeared in order to take away sins, and in him there is no sin. No one who abides in him keeps on sinning; no one who keeps on sinning has either seen him or known him. Little children, let no one deceive you. Whoever practices righteousness is righteous, as he is righteous. Whoever makes a practice of sinning is of the devil, for the devil has been sinning from the beginning. The reason the Son of God appeared was to destroy the works of the devil. No one born of God makes a practice of sinning, for God's seed abides in him; and he cannot keep on sinning, because he has been born of God" (1 John 2:29–3:9).

14. "Jesus answered him, 'Truly, truly, I say to you, unless one is born again he cannot see the kingdom of God.' Nicodemus said to him, 'How can a man be born when he is

as naturally, deep down, in the grip of sin: that is, of rebellious, anti-God pride and self-centeredness. They took it as their business to present to sinners the truth about Jesus Christ the Savior, and the reality of Christ himself, the risen, living, present Lord; to call on them to respond to the good news of grace; and to guide faithful responders to glory by drilling them in clear-headed, wholehearted discipleship to their Master.

Baxter's own *Reformed Pastor* shows what this task meant for him personally, and Mr. Great-heart in the second part of Bunyan's *Pilgrim's Progress* profiles it in broadest terms. What we call depression and Baxter called melancholy, compounded as it is of nonrationality, delusion, the sloth of inaction, and the gloom of despair, keeps its victims from thoughtful, perceptive, resolute commitment to Christ, with hope, joy, and love, that the gospel calls for. So it should seem no wonder that Baxter saw the relieving of melancholy as a major task for the pastor, nor that he should prescribe for its relief a modified version of Christian devotional disciplines.

The approach to depression, however, that marks today's Western world parts company with that of Baxter and his Puritan colleagues all along the line. To start with, the historic Christian notion of community has been replaced by a secular, pragmatic, this-worldly mind-set which takes for granted that everyone's proper goal is a pain-free, well-socialized, self-fulfilling functional efficiency in whatever style of life one may

old? Can he enter a second time into his mother's womb and be born?' Jesus answered, 'Truly, truly, I say to you, unless one is born of water and the Spirit, he cannot enter the kingdom of God. That which is born of the flesh is flesh, and that which is born of the Spirit is spirit. Do not marvel that I said to you, "You must be born again." The wind blows where it wishes, and you hear its sound, but you do not know where it comes from or where it goes. So it is with everyone who is born of the Spirit.'

"Nicodemus said to him, 'How can these things be?' Jesus answered him, 'Are you the teacher of Israel and yet you do not understand these things? Truly, truly, I say to you, we speak of what we know, and bear witness to what we have seen, but you do not receive our testimony. If I have told you earthly things and you do not believe, how can you believe if I tell you heavenly things?'" (John 3:3–12).

choose to embrace. Depression is viewed now not as a specific disorder of already disordered and misdirected human nature but as mental illness, a phenomenon on a par with physical illness, namely, the malfunctioning of an organ or process that is built into the human system. Clinical depression is a label for any state of diffused gloom and sadness that negates endeavor, achievement, and satisfaction with life, and breeds discontent and hopelessness in their place. It is nowadays linked with panic disorder, and aspects of schizophrenia and bipolar disease, as a condition that well-chosen medication should be able to relieve.

So far, no doubt, so true. My only point is that when Christians are in depression, this is not the whole story; for such depression is not ordinarily viewed as evidence that human nature in itself is fallen out of shape, nor as a reality with which pastors of churches or leaders of Christian groups are in any way qualified to deal. The assumption is that depressed persons should be guided to members of the medical, therapeutic, and helping professions, who will, it is hoped, through antidepressant drugs linked where necessary with structured counseling, succeed in restoring the victims of oppressive sadness to a life of rational, cheerful enterprise. Within this world of diagnosis and treatment all forms of religion are commonly suspect as unbalancing eccentricities, and Christian pastors in particular are in effect, sometimes explicitly, requested from time to time to keep their hands off.

Unquestionably, there is gain, within limits, in the modern development of depression therapy, but there seems to be loss too. Pastors in the Reformed, Puritan, and evangelical traditions see it as their business to keep teaching the truth about Jesus Christ, crucified and glorified, through whom the Holy Spirit will work moral-spiritual transformation in the lives of those who turn to him, seeking salvation from the guilt and power of sin. Such pastors, serving people in this way, when faced with depression will surely wish to bring at least some of the thinking that Baxter exemplifies to bear on the situation. So, does there not seem to be need for a pattern of partnership between them and those psychiatrists who do not rule out religion as an element in the good life? This question requires further discussion. But for the moment we should stand aside and let Baxter speak for himself.

## "Directions to the Melancholy" and "The Cure of Melancholy"

During his years of exclusion from the pastorate by the terms of the 1662 Act of Uniformity, Baxter, while living quietly in or near London, gained a reputation as a consultant on many spiritual disorders, melancholy being one. It should not surprise us, therefore, that when plans were made for a series of topical-textual lecture-sermons on pastoral problems, each to be given by a nonconforming clergyman and all to be published, Baxter should have been booked to preach to the question "What are the best preservatives against melancholy and overmuch sorrow?" and to do so with reference to 2 Corinthians 2:7, where the phrase "overmuch sorrow" (KJV) is found. Baxter was a treatise-minded thinker who always sought to say, however briefly, everything he knew about the topic he had in mind, and here he took the opportunity to spell out all he knew about the pastoral handling of depression in its various forms.

Twice previously (in the second "Direction" of his *Right Method for a Settled Peace of Conscience and Spiritual Comfort*; and in "Directions to the Melancholy about Their Thoughts," in his *Christian Directory*—rendered in our chap. 3 as "Advice to Depressed and Anxious Christians"), he had written an account of the melancholic condition, viewed as spiritual malfunctioning. In "The Cure of Melancholy and Overmuch Sorrow, by Faith" (rendered in our chap. 4 as "The Resolution of Depression and Overwhelming Grief through Faith"), he lays it out as a blockage to faith, hope, joy, and love. Having contextualized it as one form of "overmuch sorrow," he labors to cover all the bases of corrective and potentially curative pastoral ministration that the Bible affords.

*Chapter 2*

# RICHARD BAXTER: PERSPECTIVE AND RETROSPECTIVE

## Michael S. Lundy, MD

The works reproduced in this book reflect several decades of Richard Baxter's intense, sustained, and practical caring for people more than 350 years ago. Baxter went to great lengths to put the lessons learned down with pen and ink. He was an extraordinarily good man.[1]

A number of biographies of the Reverend Richard Baxter are available,[2] as are his own autobiographical writings,[3] with my

1. Thanks are extended to: Drs. Ligon Duncan and J. I. Packer, for their comments on my initial revision of Baxter's "Directions"; my editor, Thom Notaro, who was skillful and diplomatic; and, most of all, my wife, Robin W. Lundy, who transcribed much of the material from the original and carefully and patiently read, reread, and usefully commented on my many revisions and, as ever, proved herself an unfailing support.
2. Thoughtful and sympathetic biographies can be found online.
3. Richard Baxter and J. I. Packer, *A Grief Sanctified: Passing through Grief to Peace and Joy* (Ann Arbor, MI: Vine, 1998).

colleague and elder brother in this present labor being the real contemporary authority on Baxter. Dr. Packer's original writings give a most adequate context in which to place and appreciate Baxter and his many illustrious seventeenth-century peers.[4]

## Shepherd of Soul and Body

Baxter lived a double life—not in terms of duplicity but in function—and our two introductory chapters reflect that duality. As was perfectly allowable and evidently not uncommon in his day, Baxter was an ordained pastor who also, out of necessity, served as a lay physician. Accordingly, Dr. Packer and I write from our respective areas of professional qualification and experience, but also from our perspectives as lay counselor (J.I.P.) and lay theologian (M.S.L.). That such distinctions and caveats have to be introduced indicates a specialization in both medicine and theology that has perhaps impoverished each in certain respects. Our independent but similar interests over the years are represented in our now collaborative effort to reduce the (we say) unhelpful and often unwarranted segregation of body and soul, medical and pastoral, theological and psychological.[5] The isolation of the clinical and the pastoral has hardly been an unqualified good, and while advances in medicine have been tremendous since Baxter's day, many fundamental aspects of the practice of medicine remain—and should remain—unchanged.

Reductionist conceptualizations of body and soul are not new, and while not always inappropriate, do not always result in practical clarity, despite good-faith attempts to do so. Ef-

---

4. See J. I. Packer, *A Quest for Godliness: The Puritan Vision of the Christian Life* (Wheaton, IL: Crossway, 1990); and Packer, *The Redemption and Restoration of Man in the Thought of Richard Baxter* (Vancouver: Regent College Publishing, 2003).

5. It has been said that *distinguishing* the head from the rest of the body is one thing; *separating* the two, quite another. As this distinction is the difference between expounding and executing, we should take similar care in our treatment of the person and distinguish without separating soul and body, mind and matter.

forts to simplify the notions of body and soul date to antiquity, resulting in confusion about the nature and care of each. Efforts to repair such conceptual confusion have produced terms such an *integrative medicine, holistic care*, and so forth. These efforts are not entirely recent. My own abrupt introduction to them came from a stark example of what happens when physicians—good ones—attempt to treat the body without addressing the soul.

I was a medical student at Tulane University. A patient had been admitted to the hospital's emergency medicine service the night before. Involved in the relatively young person's care were an internal medicine intern and a resident physician. Because this patient came to the emergency room with severe and crushing substernal chest pain, she was promptly moved to the front of the queue for an angiogram (heart catheterization). The suspected diagnosis was that of "unstable angina," caused by restricted cardiac blood vessels, and this patient (not unreasonably) was deemed to be on the verge of a myocardial infarction (heart attack) if not immediately provided the only treatment thought effective at the time—emergency cardiac bypass surgery. The angiogram was required to provide the required anatomical "map" to tell the surgeon which vessels were blocked and how badly. That one or more were blocked was taken as a given, and the need for haste must have seemed equally self-evident.

To the chagrin of the resident physician and his intern, the cardiac angiogram showed a total absence of vessel narrowing. There was no radiographic evidence of the sort of heart disease expected—indeed the only sort considered. The patient's distress was deemed a straightforward presentation of cardiac disease through a misapplication of an otherwise useful principle known as Occam's razor. It was misapplied in that the list of possible causes was prematurely truncated, so that *other* underlying causes were not properly considered, much less identified.[6]

Enter George E. Burch, MD.[7] The former chairman of medicine at Tulane and a prior editor of the *American Heart Journal*, Dr. Burch was then emeritus professor of medicine and spent his time in the research laboratory as well as supervising residents, interns, and medical students. In general, Dr. Burch assumed competence in his resident physicians and used a "light hand" in matters of supervision. But he expected that confidence to be repaid with clinical diligence and intellectual rigor. Though the intern and resident had been diligent and prompt, as befitting this emergency, they for one reason or another did not obtain a complete clinical picture.

The patient (who had just undergone cardiac catheterization, a procedure then—as now—carrying significant risk) was now symptom-free and sitting up in bed to await "morning rounds," the formality by which new admissions are presented to the attending physician. Dr. Burch was properly briefed on the patient's presenting symptoms and her unremarkable prior medical history, but not on the catheterization. He pulled a chair alongside the bed and interviewed the patient for a few minutes in the presence of the resident, the intern, and two medical students attached to his service, of which I was privileged to be one. He took a focused history, which was revealing, and asked the questions that might have been asked at the time the patient arrived at the emergency room.[8]

---

6. "Occam's razor" is the principle that among competing explanations, the simplest is preferable, having the fewest assumptions. A quick overview of Occam's razor and the very different concept of scientific overdetermination will show the complexity inherent in trying to ascertain causality with confidence, one of the formidable problems in the philosophical study known as epistemology.

7. 1910–1986.

8. In fairness, this patient's presentation in the ER may not have allowed for recording an adequate history because of the acuity of her discomfort.

The patient was a woman in her late thirties, with no evident risk factors for coronary artery disease. None. However, the presenting symptoms were indistinguishable from classic angina (heart pain resulting from cardiac ischemia: a lack of oxygen owing to reduced blood flow through the coronary arteries). Yet, the history elicited by Dr. Burch provided an explanation for the patient's chest pain that the heart catheterization failed to elucidate. A story of near biblical drama unfolded in our hearing.

This young woman was the mother of three adult sons. One son had recently murdered his brother and probably faced life in prison, if not execution. The third son, enraged at what the first had done, indeed was planning to murder *him*, which would have led to the third son's incarceration and likely execution. So this parent, who had just suffered the death of one son at the hand of another, was faced with the very real prospect of losing both two remaining sons and felt powerless to prevent extension of the catastrophe. This indeed was a manifestation of heart disease: a *broken heart.*[9] This story, obtained by a skilled senior physician in a matter of three or four minutes, both provided the correct diagnosis and pointed toward the proper treatment, a treatment far more complicated yet far less dangerous than cardiac by-pass surgery.

How had this patient been so misdiagnosed and mistreated? Through an entirely sincere yet ill-advised attempt to treat her body separately from her soul, an approach that placed both at increased risk. That decision could have killed the patient as a result of the angiogram and culminated in the deaths of the remaining sons, through murder and execution. A senior physician—widely dismissed by some resident physicians as

---

9. Since then, an actual diagnosis has emerged, as well as an explanatory physiology for her symptoms: Takotsubo cardiomyopathy, also known as stress cardiomyopathy or, more descriptively, "broken heart syndrome."

out-of-date and behind the times—may have saved the lives of all three by investing less than five minutes of well-spent time.

The intense drama revealed through Dr. Burch's simple history-taking was indelibly imprinted on my mind. I wish I could say that I have always since avoided the trap of dualism and reductionism. I haven't. Nor have most of my medical colleagues. If anything, the allure of a reductionist dualism has increased, inadvertently driven by advances in technology and decreases in time spent talking with patients. Ironically, this has occurred in spite of attention given to holistic medicine under its various labels. In fact, an effort to practice holistically can, for many busy primary care physicians, become just another time-consuming documentation requirement, another box to check. The unintended consequence of well-intended efforts to solve thorny problems while asking too few questions demonstrates the aphorism that "the chief cause of problems is solutions."[10]

Dr. Burch's tutelage has kept me from losing sight of the inherent good of integrated care, and has made me leery of the marketing strategies that have come along, since his day, touting many dubious approaches, including a number of self-help remedies. A competent, intimate, and remarkably detailed biography of Dr. George Burch's wide-ranging and sometimes controversial influence on the field of clinical medicine is available.[11] I will restrict my already generous comments to this one unforgettable lesson: Each of us is far more complicated than can be explained by physiology, neurochemistry, or psychological formulation. Our very complicated physiology, neurochemistry, and psychology are all profoundly affected by our souls, even as our souls are by them.

---

10. Attributed to Eric Sevareid, long-time CBS news journalist.
11. Vivian Burch Martin, *The Celestial Society: A Life of Medicine* (Bloomington, IN: Xlibris, 2010).

Baxter wrote about the care of the soul and the care of the body as if they were indivisible if not indistinguishable components of the same person. While this is an oft-cited goal of modern medicine and has been spoken of and written about so much as to make further reference tedious, Baxter had an advantage. He actually wasn't trying to unite two divided parts of the person but saw soul and body together clearly as the person. His writing and advice reflect that.

As a postmedieval yet still premodern metaphysician, Baxter "got," in operational terms, what postmodern man is still trying to grasp. For Baxter, there was no conflict between body and soul, though he would not dispute that there was very often a real and practical *tension*—or imbalance—between them. But one gathers that encounters with either disembodied souls or soulless but still-living bodies were alien to Baxter's thought and practice as a metaphysician, either overtly or implicitly. At the same time, he had an appreciation of the tendency in his own day for patients to emphasize the soul over the body or—less often—the body over the soul. His advice is a directed and effective correction to those tendencies which, while ancient, continue to this very day and still need to be countered.

## The Seventeenth-Century Puritan

Introducing Baxter is at once pleasant and awkward. It is awkward on a couple of fronts. First, he was a Puritan, and it remains difficult to introduce Puritanism to anyone who has not already identified with that movement. My own references to Baxter as a Puritan pastor have often evoked the response "What?"—a perplexity outpacing any awareness that he lived and wrote in seventeenth-century England, a time and place of incredible turmoil. The unfortunate caricature of Puritans accepted by Christians and non-Christians has been thoroughly debunked,[12] but this debunking has been assiduously ignored by those not already sympathetic to the Puritan vision of the Christian life. So I don't always bother to mention that Baxter was a Puritan. It's just not always helpful or relevant.

It is improper, however, *not* to identify Baxter as a Puritan in the context of the edited republication of his own writings, especially as his opportunities for writing were directly related to his years of persecution for his theological and political positions as a Puritan. Being deprived of the freedom to preach, he turned to writing; and he continued to say, in writing, what he was no longer able to speak openly, following his deposition from his office. But the position of the English Puritan has been detailed in the highly readable work by Dr. Packer.[13] Those who carry an unexamined bias against the Puritans might at least wish to probe that bias in light of Packer's comments. Those already familiar with his writings are likely to be acquainted with the several other works that explore and explode the untruths that persist about these men and women.

In addition to understanding that Baxter was a Puritan, one also needs to appreciate that he was an Englishman of the seventeenth century. That was, to our modern sensibilities, a long time ago. Who could be less trendy or more easily dismissed than a long-dead, white Englishman? "Dr." Baxter is in danger of being relegated to the same category as my other mentor Dr. Burch: *out-of-date and out of touch*. This valuation proves to be even less applicable to Baxter than to Dr. Burch (who pioneered innovative and unconventional approaches, some of which remain accepted as standards of care). Now, one can ac-

---

12. The pioneering work of restoring a historical view of the Puritans is Perry Miller, *The New England Mind: The Seventeenth Century* (Boston: Beacon, 1961). See also Leland Ryken, *Worldly Saints: The Puritans as They Really Were* (Grand Rapids, MI: Zondervan, 1986).

13. Packer, *A Quest for Godliness*.

curately quibble that the medications—"physic"—commended by Baxter would not find acceptance today. And Dr. Burch's sometimes idiosyncratic suspicion of the latest drug was also legitimately criticized by his subordinates and peers. But those are anachronistic and extraneous criticisms of both men. What is relevant to each is the understanding of human nature embodied in their clinical approaches to each patient.

A number of things *have* changed since the seventeenth century. What specific psychiatric conditions are called (nomenclature) and how such conditions are classified (nosology) continue to change. Treatments for psychiatric conditions have perhaps been as varied as the names given to those conditions over the centuries. What seems to have remained unchanged, however, is the *nature* of psychiatric disorders.

If it is true that the underlying psychiatric conditions themselves have remained constant, what universal principles of general diagnosis and treatment might we find to be applicable over the ages? Are there enduring and effective approaches to alleviating suffering and misery? Or is it the general rule that the latest is also the greatest?

If history—or our understanding of it—were linear and progressive, then we would assume today's medical treatments to be *necessarily* better than yesterday's. How much more so than those of over three hundred years ago? To some degree, this is true. We no longer advocate what we regard as barbaric and ineffective treatments. Bleeding comes to mind when antiquated medical practices are mentioned. Ironically, the practice of bleeding, which was once widely applied for all manner of illnesses, has found a modern application for a very narrow range of hematologic conditions.[14] Might we find in Baxter's

---

14. For the curious, here are two examples and superficial explanations. (1) Polycythemia vera is a condition in which the body produces an excess of erythrocytes (red cells), resulting in too much of a good thing. Symptomatic treatment entails removal

writing general advice that has endured the test of time? As the recommendations he advances are themselves both general and particular, it seems reasonable to hope that sound general advice from one age may prove valid for another, though the specific applications of such advice will always require an individualized approach.

## Baxter's Terms and Our Times

It is also necessary to filter some of the terminology Baxter employs, some of which has only imprecise analogy in modern medicine and psychology. For example, the humoral theory of medicine—an ancient Greek construct derived from nonexperimental science—continued to hold sway in Baxter's time. Though it is tempting to consider this quaint at best and ignorant at worst, the categories employed as explanations of human personality and temperament in fact have rough analogies today. The lay interest in computer-based personality profiles such as the Myers-Briggs (with its four quadrants) is one example. These models are very useful tools if properly understood and employed within their inherent constraints. The humoral theory—with its four "humors" (black bile, yellow bile, phlegm, and blood) giving rise (when dominating), respectively, to melancholic, choleric, phlegmatic, and sanguine temperaments—may have been as good a fit for the science as for the existing pharmacology. While this may not seem to

---

of the excessive red cells via phlebotomy, or controlled bloodletting. This reduces the excessive viscosity of the patient's blood for a time, but as new cells are produced again in excess, the procedure must be repeated. (2) In hemochromatosis, the body retains excessive iron and stores it in organs (liver, heart), which are eventually destroyed by the iron overload. Although the affected individuals do not have excessive red cells, they may be subjected to phlebotomy in order to produce a red cell *deficiency* (anemia). Iron in the form of hemoglobin is removed via phlebotomy; mobilization of iron from stores in the liver and heart is then required to resolve the induced anemia. With time and repeated phlebotomy (and, yes, other treatments), iron can be removed from these organs to mitigate damage.

be a ringing endorsement, the outdated theory continues to provide a useful if coarse description of personality structure.

While there may be good reasons to support the notion that the incidence and prevalence of mental disorders has changed over the centuries, such fluctuation would appear more likely to be represented by increases and decreases in specific conditions, and would not be expected to influence the underlying *nature* of such illnesses. Again, the verifiable epidemic of cardiovascular diseases in the twentieth and twenty-first centuries is emblematic of this. Similarly, depression has increased dramatically, and continues to do so. However, it remains *depression*, and not some new, never-before-seen condition. The introduction of previously unheard of (and highly imaginative) conditions into the psychiatric "field guide"[15] has not gone uncontested, as cautions from serious and well-credentialed researchers reflect.[16]

Skeptics—not just cynics—have referred to the recent increase in cases of depression in the United States as the "so-called" epidemic of depression. How, they reason, can there be such a dramatic increase in conditions long known to exist but never before seen in such overwhelming numbers and spanning such a widening age range? The suspicion of some is that pharmaceutical companies and the psychiatric profession have implicitly (or even explicitly) conspired to weaken the criteria for diagnosis and thus inflate the number of cases (and people placed on medication). The actual answer to such questions of incidence and prevalence can be made rhetorically: How can we possibly be seeing more diabetes globally than was present in prior centuries? Diabetes has for many years been diagnosed and monitored by direct and indirect measurements of blood glucose. The period during

---

15. Paul McHugh, "DSM-5: A Manual Run Amok," *Wall Street Journal* (May 17, 2013).

16. Allen Frances, "The New Crisis of Confidence in Psychiatric Diagnosis," *Annals of Internal Medicine* 159, no. 3 (August 6, 2013).

which better test procedures caused an increase in the rate of detection and diagnosis has substantially passed, and epidemiologists are now justifiably confident that we are seeing an absolute increase in diabetes in Western countries. In other words, some things *have* changed, and there are varying degrees of evidence to suggest that these changes have contributed to or even caused the increases in the incidence and prevalence of age-old illnesses. It is also true that some things have not changed, and Flip Wilson's "the Devil made me do it" excuse for what would never have previously been called illness does not appear any more convincing when dressed up by the American Psychiatric Association in the form of the DSM-5.[17]

What *has* fundamentally changed is *how we live our lives*, or what is often termed *lifestyle*. What we do—what we eat, how we earn our living, what we think, how much we drink, how much sleep we get, how and on what we spend time and money, and how we treat others—all of this affects our health (and that of others) in ways still not fully understood, but to degrees long held to be important. The Puritans, among others, were aware of this and—being careful logicians and prolific writers—outlined these matters to make them more generally familiar and available. Baxter was one among many, but one whose thoughts—"directions," as he put it—have remained accessible. Though his is hardly a household name, his most important pastoral theology work, *The Reformed Pastor*, remains a revered and still-read classic in seminaries worldwide. Baxter is revered among those who know his writings for his eminently practical directions about how to adjust what we think, say, and do so as to meet biblical standards.

Nevertheless, when Baxter goes on to reference a particular humoral imbalance or composition, we are correct to avoid the

17. *Diagnostic and Statistical Manual of Mental Disorders: DSM-5*, 5th ed. (Arlington, VA: American Psychiatric Publishing, 2013).

anachronism of overlaying those ancient notions with those deriving from modern medicine and neurochemistry. Thus, an "imbalance" of the humoral system is not really equivalent to the popular notion of a "chemical imbalance" being responsible for depression, schizophrenia, or bipolar disorder, for example. On the other hand, the overly simplistic (can we say reductionist?) notion of a chemical imbalance is proving as inadequate in our day for explaining disease and guiding treatment as was the humoral theory in its lengthy heyday. Depression has been found to be much more complex than a "serotonin deficiency," as was once posited and as is often still described. The continued use of "chemical imbalance" as an explanation for a wide variety of illnesses ranging from diabetes to thyroid disease to specific psychiatric conditions conveys an illusion of understanding and of definitive causality in terms of both care and cure. Such a simplicity, however, is to be found in none of these conditions, though a definitive treatment may be standard procedure for these same conditions. For example, if diabetes is conceptualized as a deficiency of insulin—which may or may not be the case—then the false expectation is advanced that the condition and its numerous sequelae (cardiovascular disease, peripheral neuropathy, kidney disease, eye disease, etc.) can be controlled or prevented simply by "just the right dose" of insulin. The same notion of getting on the "right medication" has proved similarly inadequate as a construct with regard to psychiatric conditions.

Insistence upon choosing either the old or the new constitutes a false dilemma. It is the appropriate *mixing* of the old and the new that constitutes wisdom, as Christ himself taught (Matt. 13:52).[18] And so it is in the diagnosis and treatment of

---

18. "And he said to them, 'Therefore every scribe who has been trained for the kingdom of heaven is like a master of a house, who brings out of his treasure what is new and what is old'" (Matt. 13:52).

depression and anxiety. Therefore, it should not be surprising that some of the newer and more effective treatments for these conditions do—often unwittingly—echo approaches outlined by Richard Baxter so long ago. It is not that there are no dilemmas or that all seeming dichotomies are false, but rather that many situations are complicated and require prudence.

In the domains of both body and soul, "the right medications" are often absolutely essential but are as often only partially effective.[19] Indeed, there may be several valid and effective permutations of "the right medication," as well. Thus, medications are regularly *necessary* but not as often *sufficient* to restore or maintain well-being, and, it seems, even counterproductive if not combined with the other necessary "ingredients."[20]

This returns us to Baxter and Burch. What does each offer in terms of diagnosis and prescriptive "ingredients" that may be missing from current approaches taken by modern medicine at large, but also by both psychological and pastoral counseling? I suggest that Baxter and Burch—from very different eras, backgrounds, and philosophical orientations—each carried a unified and complex understanding of the individual in terms of both a general human nature and specific familial, cultural, and

19. "Just the right dose" was Dr. Burch's reply to his medical students' anxious attempts to calculate an overly precise quantity of insulin for a particular patient in response to Burch's query, "How much insulin does a diabetic need?" He wished to convey that the "right dose" was highly dependent on who was being treated and could not be adequately expressed simply in units of insulin based merely on the patient's blood glucose level at some arbitrary time. That is, he demanded that the patient be viewed as a unique person, and not reduced to a set of laboratory values. This comment and many more were captured in *The Quotations of Chairman George*, informally published by the Tulane University School of Medicine graduating class of 1974 in appreciation of Dr. Burch's influence.

20. There *are* cases in which "mere" medication appears sufficient to work a magic so complete and comprehensive as to obviate the need for complementary interventions. However, these situations are rare, and the notion that a bare medication could be prescribed in the absence of the sort of encouraging and supportive patient-physician relationship necessary to its proper use is risible. Although difficult to measure, the *context* in which a medication is prescribed and taken is probably as important as the raw pharmacology of the medication itself.

spiritual attributes. Today, we might use terms such as *strength* and *weakness*, *vulnerability* and *resilience*, *diathesis* and *protective factors*, *positive* and *negative influences*, and so forth. And each man knew when a little information was sufficient to allow the safe disregard of the vast information hidden behind unasked questions. A gunshot wound requires immediate action and demands a relatively constrained set of questions, answers to which may be available only from a technical (e.g., surgical) approach in the care of an unconscious, unaccompanied victim of trauma. It would be absurd to postpone emergency trauma surgery to obtain a detailed social history! Yet, preventing the next incident may well entail eliciting such a history from the stabilized and eventually responsive patient.

Baxter, in this sense, understands critical priorities in the care of the soul. He grasps, for example, that the threat of suicide is a matter of such urgency that it *must* be interrupted, if at all possible, and the individual protected from self-destruction. Logic is a strong suit of Puritan thinking and living, and Baxter makes good use of it. He understands and explains cause and effect, distinguishes primary conditions from secondary complications, and is seemingly at home with a degree of complexity that might overwhelm many of us in the twenty-first century.

## Whence This Wisdom?

What are the components of Baxter's wisdom? Where are they to be located?[21] Put simply, they are to be found in the Puritan theology that Baxter and his colleagues preached and practiced.

---

21. Cf. Job 28:12:

> But where shall wisdom be found?
> And where is the place of understanding?"

Job provides God's answer:

> Behold, the fear of the Lord, that is wisdom,
> and to turn away from evil is understanding.

And the efforts of disciplined, individual application of theology logically preceded the preaching of it. Not many respected Puritan pastors would dare to preach very far—if at all—in advance of their own experience and some measure of success in implementing the advice they publicly offered to others. Thus, not only can it be assumed that Baxter's pastoral and clinical approaches are rigorously informed by an undergirding theology and metaphysical philosophy; it is also evident that both personal and professional experience guided his written advice.

One is wont to ask, where did this man get such wisdom? For Baxter, the answer is not easy. He was prolific in recording in detail what was conventional wisdom among his pastoral peers. But where did he obtain those elements of his wisdom that we claim to be so enduring and relevant in the twenty-first century? Part of the answer is that scholars and practitioners alike in the seventeenth century borrowed and exchanged ideas freely. These ideas were rarely attributed to their original sources, with notable exceptions.

As one might expect, Baxter's practical advice is intrinsically and deeply biblical, and this is reflected in both explicit and implicit references to biblical passages and to the deeply Calvinistic theology common to the Puritans. When alluding to a particular passage, Baxter may provide an actual reference, but he as often assumes a degree of biblical familiarity that is rare today, though ubiquitous in his extended circles. He may well employ the historic rabbinical practice of citing a mere fragment of a lengthy passage, with the fragment intended to serve as shorthand for the whole (and understood to do so by his readers).

An ancient precedent would be the many times Jesus referenced snippets of Old Testament verses—often from the Psalms—which his hearers would know to represent the larger text, and which would accordingly be understood in the context of that entire but largely unspoken passage. A more recent example is the novel *Moby-Dick: or, The Whale.* While one can read the novel and enjoy it to some degree even if ignorant of Old Testament Scriptures, it is impossible—so I was once advised[22]—to grasp the multiple and nested scriptural allusions that Melville—*not a Christian*—employed in this famous American novel unless one is steeped in the Old Testament. Melville expects a high degree of biblical literacy from his readers, a reasonable expectation in his day.

Baxter assumes a similar familiarity with biblical texts and with theological constructs. His footnotes are few. But the theology—or system of thinking—developed and embraced by the Puritans is much larger than a narrowly biblical base. While the Bible is the absolute, carefully examined basis for faith and life among Baxter and his many colleagues, in practical terms he and they borrowed widely from many sources, and used Aristotelian principles of logic, which they made to conform to Christian theology.

It is Baxter's deeply and carefully articulated Christian theology coupled with his adaptation of Stoic moral philosophy that makes his work so enduring and compelling. The Puritans unabashedly took what they could from a variety of sources, holding that all truth was ultimately from God, and that such truth as was revealed to ancient pagans through general revelation could be legitimately recycled, with care, and applied in an explicitly Christian context.

What emerges in Baxter's material is a curious and compelling mixture of sound Christian doctrines and general holistic medical principles, applying reframed Stoic concepts to those

---

22. Classroom communication from Rev. Graham Hales, "Introduction to Religion" (University of Southern Mississippi, 1976). My own subsequent, if belated, reading of this American classic abundantly confirmed my teacher's assertion.

doctrines and principles, and formulated as irrefutable logic. Baxter's use of logic was characteristic of the highly educated clergy of his day. The Stoics had numerous ideas that were antithetical to Christian belief and practice, such as suicide;[23] that did not keep the Puritans from appreciating those elements of the Stoics' philosophy which were general and adaptable to Christian thought. Specifically, the logical beliefs and practices articulated so carefully by the Stoics were repurposed—as we now say—by Baxter and his ilk, with very pointed examples in the material to follow.[24]

Logic for Baxter (and his contemporaries) was a practical exercise far advanced from the Logic 101 some of us may have encountered in college and then forgotten. Belief and behavior were inextricably linked for Baxter, as they were for the Stoics. What you believed determined how you thought about matters and predetermined how you would respond to possible choices along the path of life. Distorted beliefs would inevitably lead to wrong interpretations of circumstances and so to wrong choices and unethical behavior.

Baxter is at pains to use logic to critique, challenge, comfort, and cajole his readers. While he doesn't explicitly tell you what he's doing or even why, he has no compunctions about painting you into a corner with his interrogatories and then asking you what you want to do next. He's fond of reducing a seemingly intractable matter to a binary choice. And his reasoning is theologically as well as logically sound. Like his contemporaries, he does not sense any need to credit anyone with ideas borrowed

---

23. Epictetus clearly alludes to suicide, for example, as an acceptable if regrettable way to escape an otherwise intractable moral dilemma. See *The Teaching of Epictetus Being the "Enchiridion of Epictetus," with Selections from the "Dissertations" and "Fragments,"* available as a free Amazon Kindle book.

24. The purported influence of Stoic philosophy on the Puritan mind is largely undocumented and represents a fertile area of research (J. I. Packer, personal communication to M. S. Lundy, May 25, 2016).

from others (e.g., Epictetus) and adapted for his purposes. The sort of obsessive attribution and citations that one expects to encounter nowadays in scholarly works was quite uncommon in Baxter's day, and throughout history until recently. Not only were there no copyright laws; the notion of a proprietary ownership of material made available to the public as a part of one's duties seems to have been absent. So Baxter—formally equipped though largely self-taught in logic as well as in Hebrew, Greek, and Latin—felt perfectly at ease with employing that training. It was simply the right and practical thing to do.

Ironically, Baxter's own approach to what we would label depression, anxiety, or psychosis has gone unrecognized and therefore uncredited by twentieth- and twenty-first-century clinicians who have used similar approaches from a secular perspective. What Baxter employed was a clear forerunner of what we now call cognitive-behavioral therapy (CBT). His version of CBT would be deemed rudimentary and highly tailored to his relatively homogenous clinical population. Yet, it must still be recognized as a forerunner of a very powerful and highly respected tool for dealing with many otherwise intractable clinical problems, particularly those of a severe and chronic nature, including the aforementioned ones.

Baxter begins by advising his readers to get their personal theology straight, goes on to tell them how practically to do that using his own antecedent to CBT, and makes sure that his readers understand that their problems have somatic as well as emotional and spiritual dimensions. Then he concludes by telling his readers to trust their physicians and to take their medicines! Describing this as a confluence of belief, behavior, and medicine oversimplifies Baxter's approach but is a good synopsis for those willing to explore the sort of advice he so freely gives.

## Help for the Hurting

With all due respect to those self-improvement books which *are* useful (when they are modest and limited in scope): this is *not* a self-help book in the conventional sense,[25] though it is certainly intended to be *helpful*. Baxter writes from that perspective and commends his readers first to the care of their faithful Savior, Jesus Christ, and then to the care of faithful friends and family, along with "familiar"[26] physicians. So to those who read Baxter's advice—here provided in language more accessible to our present literary sensibilities—I commend the same.

If Baxter's advice is read and even followed without a deeply embraced understanding of the Christian faith he assumes to be present in most of his readers, it would then be unreasonable to hold Baxter at fault for the failure of his good advice. Since we are dealing with a very English, if politically incorrect—then and now, actually and metaphorically—guide in Baxter, an English aphorism may be excused. It has been said that the Battle of Waterloo was won on the playing fields of Eton—a statement with a lot of baggage but perhaps a real point.[27] Baxter's formulations, diagnoses (in the general sense), and advice cannot be either understood or properly applied without a fairly good alignment with Baxter's theological beliefs. That is,

---

25. The irreverent and hilarious book by Walker Percy, *Lost in the Cosmos—The Last Self-Help Book* (New York: Farrar, Straus & Giroux, 1983) pillories the notion of self-help while alluding to the availability of genuine help in a manner best left to Dr. Percy's own words and style.

26. What Baxter appears to have in mind is the family physician who has served a family well and faithfully over several generations, and is thus well-acquainted with the patient and his circumstances. Baxter would have *known* such physicians during his upbringing in rural England, and he would have emulated them during the years when he practiced medicine on an emergency basis in the parish of Kidderminster.

27. Matthew Arnold comments: "The aged Barbarian [i.e., a member of the English upper classes] will, upon this, mumble to us his story how the battle of Waterloo was won in the playing-fields of Eton. Alas! disasters have been prepared in those playing-fields as well as victories; disasters due to inadequate mental training—to want of application, knowledge, intelligence, lucidity" ("Misquotation: 'The battle of Waterloo was won on the playing fields of Eton,'" *Oxford Academic*, August 8, 2013, http://oupacademic .tumblr.com/post/57740288322/misquotation-the-battle-of-waterloo-was-won-on).

don't expect to win the battle if you have not put in time doing the preparatory work. Even then, it will still be a difficult and uncertain struggle. And lack of preparation may be preparation for disaster.

Baxter assumes a basically Christian orientation in his readers, and addresses them as theologically Reformed and biblically grounded. He does not require his readers to be trained theologians, but does expect them to be receptive to the theological concepts he uses to make arguments and provide directions.

Baxter believes in a loving, generous God, but doubts that his readers adequately appreciate just *how* good God really is. Baxter approaches some of his readers as doubting God's goodness, or their own ability to benefit from it (which is a doubt of God's greatness). He attacks these and other areas of unbelief vigorously.

Yet, Baxter is himself kind and generous to those who are debilitated and unable to think clearly or rationally, or much at all.[28] These he commends not to complex or extended meditation, lengthy prayers, fasting, strict asceticism, or the like, but to the care of their friends and family; he expressly limits such patients' efforts to do what they are unable—out of disability—to do.

Baxter's appreciation that a diminished capacity reduces culpability is, I think, consistent with established legal precedents in English common law of the time, which remain valid today. Yet he does not permit a *particular* inability to license a *general* unwillingness, or excuse his readers for failing to do what they *can* do on the grounds that they can *not* do *all* that they *should* or *would* do. Here the parable of the talents is brought to mind: having few resources may reduce the demands for

---

28. Heb. 5:1: "For every high priest chosen from among men is appointed to act on behalf of men in relation to God, to offer gifts and sacrifices for sins." Baxter is clearly modeling his own attitudes by his High Priest's example.

our performance without eliminating the requirement that we diligently discharge our duties as we *are* able.[29]

So, what is the value of reading Baxter if we are insufficiently grounded in the Bible and the Reformed theology—biblical theology—which Baxter assumes? Much in every way.[30] For the Christian reader—imagined to be the one more likely to pick up this work—there is to be found in Baxter a breadth of advice applicable to a great range of biblical and theological sophistication. For the learned, much will resonate. For those less well versed, Baxter proves as interested in challenging and teaching as in assuming agreement or full comprehension. Overall, Baxter sees part of his work—for sophisticated as well as for less informed readers—as drawing them into a dialogue and then identifying and challenging misconceptions, and then assisting in charting a new direction based on corrected assumptions. He is more directive than some modern practitioners of CBT would allow—but that is his style and burden as a pastor. He's not ashamed to share what he knows and believes or to use it to shape others' expectations of themselves.

## The Risk of Isolating Blame

I grew up spiritually at a time when the very notion of mental illness tended to be looked upon with suspicion in some religious circles. Any doubts I had about mental illnesses being diseases of the brain were confronted by compelling reality during my medical training. If anything, my doubts may have tilted toward a conviction that such conditions represented *only* diseases of the brain and not of the soul. Having had serial

---

29. One of my former pastors and favorite teachers, Mark E. Ross (MDiv, PhD), was fond of saying, with regard to theological understanding, "Don't let what you *don't know* confuse you about what you *do know*." By extension, we should not let what we *cannot* do stand in the way of the things we *can* do.

30. To borrow Paul's phrase from Rom. 3:2.

run-ins with reality during my training, research, and practice, I now imagine myself to hold a more nuanced view of such matters. Basically, I think I know more than I once did but a lot less than I once thought I knew. Life, death, joy, sadness, suffering, and illness have each proved to be much more complicated than I once believed.

One of the reasons I appreciate Baxter so much is that he lived and wrote at a time when such complexities were givens—not exceptions—of every day for everyone. While some lived then as long as we do now, on average most did not. Illness and suffering and premature death were commonplace and could not be eliminated through any available remedy. Treatments existed, to be sure, with the cure of the soul thought to offer the most hopeful outcome, but one recognized as fulfilled only partially in this life. Our society's efforts to change this situation by eradicating visible manifestations of sickness, suffering, and even nonconformity, while meeting with technical success, cannot all be said to be ending well. The eradication of smallpox and the prospect of doing the same for polio are indisputable goods. The declining incidence of Down syndrome births, at least in the West, and the increasing male-to-female birth disparity in the East represent abuses of technology and carry hideous moral costs. Yet, our efforts, expenditures, and even moral compromises cannot rid our world of many of the afflictions common to us all.

Meanwhile, denial remains one of the most popular and—when appropriately utilized—most effective short-term mechanisms for dealing—or, rather, *not* dealing—with serious personal problems, including intractable illness. As applied to psychiatric disorders, the somewhat narrow circle I inhabited as a young person (and younger Christian) espoused a form of denial alongside peculiar assertions. Mental illness specifically was often denied as such, while the undeniable manifestations of it were regularly attributed either to sin or to the direct working of the Devil or his minions (i.e., demons). But misdiagnosis leads to mistreatment, and that to a cascading set of problems, and this is a case in point.

If, on the one hand, someone's symptoms and behaviors are wrongly attributed to willful and sinful proclivities and decisions that the person could resist, two false purposes are served. First, it absolves the observing community of the responsibility of coming alongside the individual in a supportive capacity, and may serve to allow the community (i.e., local church), in "good faith," to pressure the afflicted member until he has "repented" or "gotten serious" about his faith. Second, if the individual buys into this formulation, he is in a terrific bind. He is urged to repent of his many obvious and secret sins, with the promise that if he does, he will receive relief from his symptoms. In many settings, the sufferer does—at least initially—accept the premise[31] and attempts a soul-searching repentance in expectation of a soul-delivering release from torment. If and when this fails to give relief, he then attempts to repent of imaginary sins that neither he nor anyone else can identify.[32]

If the symptoms that the person experiences are, in fact, the direct consequences of ongoing and unforsaken sin, then well and good. In such cases, the diagnosis and treatment correspond to reality, and immediate and sustained progress may be expected and evident.

---

31. —an action to which Job's friends repeatedly urged him, but which he wisely and rightly refused to take.

32. Dr. Packer provides a gripping account of his own nearly disastrous struggle with this sort of well-intended but bad advice, in his recollections of his search for "true consecration." It is notable that he found release from bad theology when he discovered the Puritans and their sound theology. See J. I. Packer, introduction to *On Temptation and the Mortification of Sin in Believers*, by John Owen (Vancouver: Regent College Publishing, 2014), i. It would not be unfair to say that Job's friends offered counsel similar to that of Dr. Packer's early Christian associates.

However, in cases of overt clinical depression, bipolar disorder, severe anxiety that is physiologically driven, or the psychoses, repentance may be just as necessary—who can say, "I am free from sin?"[33]—but ineffective in addressing the symptoms. Here, one is reminded of Jesus's disciples, who upon seeing the man born blind, asked, "Rabbi, who sinned, this man or his parents, that he was born blind?"[34] Clearly, they assumed his condition was someone's fault, and that fault was taken for granted to be very proximate, with only two possibilities: *he* or *his parents* had done something to deserve this. Now, we know that, at least according to Paul's commentary about Jacob and Esau—who before birth were *both* held guiltless, having done nothing good or bad[35]—this particular man's blindness could not have been the result of a sin he committed before he was born. And since he was *born* blind, it is difficult to attribute his blindness at birth to a sin he would commit as an adult. Without going into the theory of it, Jesus simply dismissed *both* of the options presented by the disciples. "Neither," is Jesus's surprising answer, meaning not that neither sinned, since we know that "all have sinned,"[36] but rather that *neither's sin was directly responsible for the specific suffering the man experienced.*

Was the blind man free of sin? Certainly not, and Jesus elsewhere extends the forgiveness of a man's sin *before* healing his body. Such an ordering, as chronicled by Matthew,[37] does not prove a logical causality between a particular sin or pattern of sinful behavior and a particular malady, but rather

---

33. Cf. Prov. 20:9.
34. John 9:2.
35. Rom. 9:11: ". . . though they were not yet born and had done nothing either good or bad."
36. Rom. 3:23.
37. Matt. 9:2: "And behold, some people brought to him a paralytic, lying on a bed. And when Jesus saw their faith, he said to the paralytic, 'Take heart, my son; your sins are forgiven.'"

acknowledges the nature of sin and its role in the general condition of mankind.

When Jesus asks, "Which is easier, to say, 'Your sins are forgiven,' or to say, 'Rise and walk'?"[38] he demonstrates that our most desperate need is for *forgiveness*. And, in contrast, the efficacious pronouncing of absolution from sin is far harder than even restoring sight to the blind.[39] But Jesus maintains the link between sin and sickness without allowing the sort of shallow causal inferences so popular in his day and ours. In fact, in a different setting, after healing a man at the Pool of Bethesda, Jesus offers him the preventive advice, "sin no more, that nothing worse may happen to you."[40] So this whole business of sin and sickness should make for a great deal of humility. We should be very hesitant either to blame others' sickness on their particular sin or to hold them entirely blameless when we are short of the sort of vision allotted to Christ.

## Assessing Causes with Humility and Compassion

So, are psychiatric illnesses the result of sin or not? Are individuals to blame, or are they not responsible for their fate? Going back to Jesus's own pronouncements and those explanations we find elsewhere in Scripture, there are connections between sin and sickness, but we are often given to see only certain layers of those links. It is true that the principles set forth in the book of Proverbs and elsewhere in the Bible suggest that right living, *generally speaking*, will lead to, shall we say, a less

---

38. Matt. 9:5.

39. Chrysostom (as quoted by Aquinas, *Summa theologica* III, q. 44, art. 3, ad. 3) says regarding Matt. 9:5: "By how much a soul is of more account than a body, by so much is the forgiving of sins a greater work than healing the body; but because the one is unseen He does the lesser and more manifest thing in order to prove the greater and more unseen." So, reasoning from the lesser to the greater, Jesus's question is self-answering. That no one bothered to ask, "Who can heal *illness* but God alone?" is supportive of this viewpoint.

40. John 5:14.

complicated existence than will ignoring those precepts. It is just as true that many of the laments and petitions in the Bible concern the seeming *exceptions* to those general principles. The wicked prosper[41] and the innocent are swept away for reasons that are perplexing without the light of special revelation, and still unsettling even in that light.[42]

We are, therefore, counseled to grapple with complexity.[43] We should be open to more nuanced answers and refrain from restricting our questions to those that require prearranged binary responses: "Is it lawful to pay taxes to Caesar, or not?"[44] "Who sinned, this man or his parents?"[45] For the latter question, we can be certain that both that man and his parents sinned, as did Job. We can, in those specific examples, be as certain that their sin was *not* directly responsible for the suffering that came their way. We are certain in those cases—and not others—because of direct revelation from God himself: "It was not that this man sinned, or his parents, but that the works of God might be displayed in him."[46] And for Job, it was his *righteousness* that brought his suffering, as the introduction to the book makes clear.[47]

It is rare that we find such direct, unequivocal disavowal of any link between specific sin and horrific suffering. It is less rare but still uncommon that specific links between particular

---

41. See Psalm 73.
42. Isa. 57:1–2:

The righteous man perishes,
   and no one lays it to heart;
devout men are taken away,
   while no one understands.
For the righteous man is taken away from calamity;
   he enters into peace.

43. Eccles. 7:18: "It is good that you should take hold of this, and from that withhold not your hand, for the one who fears God shall come out from both of them."
44. Matt. 22:17.
45. John 9:2.
46. John 9:3.
47. Job 1:8: "And the LORD said to Satan, 'Have you considered my servant Job, that there is none like him on the earth, a blameless and upright man, who fears God and turns away from evil?'"

sins and illnesses are provided. Miriam's leprosy, the shriveling of a king's arm, the death of an infant owing to the parents' sins—these and others are given as examples in the Bible.[48] But for the most part, we are left with the much more general sense that sickness and suffering in the world are distributed in ways that defy our comprehension. If ever we imagine we've figured out God's economy, it is helpful to consider the "reward" meted out to a child who *does* find favor in God's sight: he dies *because he has God's favor* and *because of God's kindness*![49] In human terms, it is often the deliberate cruelty of one person or group that causes untold suffering for others. One man sins— many other (relatively) innocent suffer. Surely, when we face the suffering of individuals, we do well to avoid confidently asserting causes and assigning personal blame—*most of the time*. Similarly, we should be hesitant to extend glib absolution that may be as ill-advised and off the mark. We are not responsible for our genetics. On the one hand, some genetic conditions are so hard-coded that the mere possession of a particular gene is destiny. Huntington's Chorea (HC) is merely one example. On the other hand, other genetic propensities are better viewed less fatalistically. Much of the struggle in the practice of medicine entails the tension between propensity toward certain diseases and personal proclivities that may lead to the activation of latent genes and expressions of disease—or, conversely, may delay or even prevent illness, or at least perhaps bring about a remission.

The determination of causality should not become a goal in and of itself. Causality itself may be obscured by other factors that sustain and aggravate symptoms. To cite a simple example: Chronic insomnia may have a very specific and identifiable

---

48. Numbers 12; 1 Kings 13.
49. 1 Kings 14 tells the story.

onset and cause. But with the passing of time, the cause tends to fade in memory, either naturally or (in the case of combat trauma, for example) because that memory is willingly or otherwise suppressed. Mind-sets that aid in the suppression of such memories, including hypervigilance, avoidance, and emotional numbing, may become habitual and outlast any deliberate or involuntary suppression or recall of those memories by decades. In such situations, the insomnia may appear to be primary (i.e., without evident cause), while yet having a very specific cause. Side effects of chronic insomnia (fatigue, irritability, poor concentration, expectation and fear of not being able to sleep) only serve to sustain and aggravate the insomnia. When, after some effort, the putative cause is identified (and this is not as common as one might wish), this finding does not magically resolve the insomnia, in that it has seemingly acquired a life of its own, with a constellation of other symptoms that confuse matters. If something with a clear chronology and convincing causality like this can be so complicated to unravel and treat, how much more are conditions in which matters of volition and genetics, guilt and innocence, and seeming happenstance coalesce? Again, with regard to causality and inferred responsibility, humility is more useful than hubris, and the rewards of the former are much more agreeable in any event.

It cannot be overemphasized that suffering is ubiquitous and is even guaranteed to those who seek to live a consciously Christian life,[50] as well as promised to those who ignore God and his kindness. Some may for a time seem to escape hardship, and may seem to do so in spite of richly deserving it,[51] but such respite, we are assured and know from general observation as

---

50. 2 Tim. 3:12: "Indeed, all who desire to live a godly life in Christ Jesus will be persecuted."

51. See Psalm 73.

well as Scripture, is transient.[52] But if the corrupt seem for a time to escape justice, and if the comparatively innocent suffer, how are we to apportion responsibility for the suffering we encounter in our own lives and in others'? *Very carefully and with humility and compassion.* Most of us know what it's like to escape many well-deserved consequences as well as to endure undeserved tribulations, what can seem like "the slings and arrows of outrageous fortune."[53] My own experience—and I know it to be true of others as well—is that we usually get a lot more breaks than we deserve, whereas we all know those whose plights seem reversed. Trying to figure out why is vexing, and sometimes unwise. So, while we cannot but emphasize that suffering comes unbidden and in forms quite unexpected and seemingly ill-fitting, we can take some solace in knowing it is the plight of mankind. Trying to explain it in too great detail or with a level of precision not supported by evidence is presumptuous, if not dangerous. So here perhaps it is best, like Augustine, to say we don't know as often as we might wish, and that we would not understand as much as we imagine even were we to know.[54]

Even in a situation as clear-cut as the HC gene, knowing (as is now possible) that one has inherited the gene and is thus doomed to develop early dementia and loss of function does not

---

52. 1 Tim. 5:24–25: "The sins of some people are conspicuous, going before them to judgment, but the sins of others appear later. So also good works are conspicuous, and even those that are not cannot remain hidden."

53. William Shakespeare, *Hamlet*, act 3, scene 1.

54. Augustine, *Confessions* 11.12.14:

> Behold, I answer to him who asks, "What was God doing before He made heaven and earth?" I answer not, as a certain person is reported to have done facetiously (avoiding the pressure of the question), "He was preparing hell," saith he, "for those who pry into mysteries." It is one thing to perceive, another to laugh,—these things I answer not. For more willingly would I have answered, "I know not what I know not," than that I should make him a laughing-stock who asketh deep things, and gain praise as one who answereth false things. (*NPNF*[1], vol. 1)

So we seek not to answer the problem of suffering but to acknowledge its universality and to say, "We know not" why it is distributed as it is.

excuse a fatalistic application of that knowledge. To be sure, the onset of clinical illness in such a case will diminish both capacity and responsibility. Yet, prior to such an onset, the to-be-affected individual still has a life to live and free choices to make. And HC represents one of the most compelling genetic cause-and-effect relationships. What about the conditions that Baxter addresses?

This expiative consideration of cause and effect, culpability and capacity, determinism and freedom is taken up repeatedly by Baxter in the form of advice he gives. Cognizant of the tension between loosely linked causes and effects, he seems to refuse to blame people for what *they cannot help*, while simultaneously refusing to acquit people of certain duties *they can and must discharge*. In the middle, he requires friends and family to do what the ailing souls cannot be expected to do themselves, yet demands of them what they alone can deliver. Baxter is at the same time gentle and difficult, generous and demanding.[55]

## As Is Common to Man

So, how do we sum up and get on to letting Baxter speak for himself? By acknowledging that the disorders he references—like those evident today—are both common and widespread, and often viewed with too narrow a focus.

Depression, bipolar disorder, schizophrenia, and a number of related and divergent conditions affect both the most reckless

---

55. A seemingly contradictory set of scriptural admonitions in Gal. 6:2–5 makes sense only in this context of shared and individual responsibility. Paul says: "Bear one another's burdens, and so fulfill the law of Christ. For if anyone thinks he is something, when he is nothing, he deceives himself. But let each one test his own work, and then his reason to boast will be in himself alone and not in his neighbor. For each will have to bear his own load." The first and last sentences refer, respectively, to overwhelming, crushing loads that cannot be born alone, and to individual duties that no one can carry out and discharge for us. We should not confuse the two (Classroom communication from Dr. Glenn C. Knecht [Fourth Presbyterian Church, Bethesda, MD, 2003]).

and the most sober-minded of individuals, Christians and non-Christians alike. To the Christian, Baxter offers not easy answers but simple solutions that, while challenging to implement, may yield the sought-after "help in time of need."[56]

Baxter offers no panaceas; he appreciates suffering as intrinsic to this life. Yet, he refuses despair, and demands of his readers—patients and caregivers alike—an optimism grounded in his view of a good and great God, and buttressed by his own very practical advice on how one can give or receive help that reflects love for God and neighbor. Baxter is neither glib nor naïve—he is, though, a man of conviction and assumes his readers are as well, or at least want to be. His advice can coax us toward the convictions he advances to us on credit.

Part of what attracted me to psychiatry was the recognition—in retrospect—of fellow believers who were suffering from a variety of conditions, ranging from schizophrenia to anxiety disorders. At the time, those individuals had been provided Christian counsel that—while well-intended—was often so far off the mark as to be harmful.

My experience as a medical student on the admission unit of a university hospital gave me a measure of optimism—unwarranted, I found—that medication could have worked near miracles for those tormented souls, the memory of which still haunts me. Subsequent experience gave me a more realistic vision—still optimistic—of what treatment can and cannot accomplish. Baxter, whom I encountered later in my career than I might have wished, has provided us with a hard-earned and practical wisdom. He knew well what I am still learning.

Dr. Burch's patient might have been prejudicially dismissed as "hysterical" or "psychosomatic" if the history had been taken early on without the compassion necessary to under-

---

56. To borrow a phrase from Heb. 4:16.

stand what was really at stake. And, of course, I wonder years later what actually happened to that mother and her sons. The diagnosis proved easy; the cure, if it came, could not have been so simple.

Tolstoy's oft-quoted statement "Happy families are all alike; every unhappy family is unhappy in its own way"[57] is, in my estimate, off the mark. When things break—including brains—there is a recognizable sameness and therefore *diagnosable* pattern in that breakage. That is not to say the breakage is simple to describe or repair. A shattered vase—no matter how lovely when intact—manifests complexity in its state of increased entropy, if one is concerned with its repair rather than its disposal. Surely, we as human beings, can be very complicated to repair. There is a sameness in the metaphorical breakage one sees in ruined lives, most conspicuously displayed in the faces and behaviors of the homeless we so carefully (and callously?) protect from coercive care.

But one sees a predictable sameness in upright and functional members of society and in the church when those lives have been disrupted by depression, unrelenting worry, psychosis, or distorted perception. Recognition of the breakage is fairly straightforward, which is one reason I think Tolstoy got it wrong. *Happiness and health manifest a much greater variety and a higher granularity of texture than does illness.*

Sorting out how to address the breakage with a realistic hope is more difficult. The rush for "the right medication" is just as overreaching as have been prior purely psychological formulations, or purely "spiritual" ones. A naïve optimism is unlikely to weather the difficulties of the repair work, and that can lead in turn to despair. An informed understanding of what

---

57. Leo Tolstoy, *Anna Karenina*, trans. Constance Garnett (various publishers), chap. 1, line 1.

must be attempted, and perhaps accomplished, better positions patients, physicians, pastors, family, and friends for what often proves to be "enduring to the end."[58]

Baxter, again, has been there. Some of his advice is for those on the brink of despair who must be turned back. Some is for those who are too comfortable with their own attitudes and thus not motivated to deal with a situation simply because it is *not yet* a crisis. Other advice is for those involved onlookers—family and friends—who must be educated about both their own obligations to the patient and the limits of those responsibilities.

This is complicated business. The philosophical conservatism implicit in Baxter's sentiments suggests an awareness of those difficulties. It is always harder to improve a situation than to make things worse. Yet he does not allow us an inactivity based on fatalism, or excuse a frozen indecisiveness. There are things that must be said and done, and while the outcome is not guaranteed, the need compels a judicious and metered response despite that uncertainty.

While it should perhaps go without saying, it will not go unsaid here: This book is not published as either a diagnostic manual or a treatment guide. It is intended to inform and enlarge the perspective of both laity and clergy, patients (and families) and professionals. Those who find themselves sympathetic to the advice Baxter offers should take his opening and closing words of "Advice to Depressed and Anxious Christians" very seriously. To paraphrase: *see to the condition of your own soul, and consult with your own pastor and your own physician, and apply their advice as appropriate.*

Baxter is a faithful friend and companion to patient, pastor, friend, family, and physician alike. He extends help that

---

58. Matt. 10:22; 24:13.

sometimes comes as pithy and pointed criticism (which may encourage us to be as direct when appropriate); at other times he exudes a warm compassion that should serve to soften our own tendencies to harshness. It is my sincere hope that Richard Baxter becomes a friend to you and yours, as he has been to me.

# PART 2

BAXTER'S COUNSEL
ON DEPRESSION

*Chapter 3*

# ADVICE TO DEPRESSED
# AND ANXIOUS
# CHRISTIANS

Richard Baxter[1]

Individuals already prone to melancholy[2] are easily and frequently thrown even more deeply into it through undisciplined patterns of thinking or unchecked emotions. The predicament of these individuals is so very sad that I believe it necessary to

---

1. Edited and updated by Michael S. Lundy, MD, from Baxter's original "Directions to the Melancholy about Their Thoughts," in *A Christian Directory*.

2. Baxter employs the still-useful term *melancholy*. His use includes a fairly broad number of psychiatric conditions that, today, are more precisely but not necessarily more accurately classified. *Melancholy* (elsewhere referred to as melancholia), as he uses it, includes depression, bipolar disorder, anxiety disorders, and psychotic disorders. As a concession to the modern reader, I will employ the term *depression* in some of the situations where Baxter used *melancholy*. My purpose in modernizing the language of Mr. Baxter is to remove certain words that have become obscure and to restructure sentences to accommodate those of us who have more difficulty holding on to multiple strands of thought than did the mighty Puritans.

give some specific advice written especially for them.[3] I encounter persons who are unacquainted with the nature of this and other diseases, and who thus greatly dishonor the name of God and bring the profession of religion into scorn. They do so by attributing all the behavior and words of melancholy persons to great and exceptional workings of the Spirit of God.[4] They then make inferences about the methods and workings of God upon the soul, as well as about the nature of influence that the Devil is allowed to exercise. Others have published the prophecies, possessions (by demons), and exorcisms of hysterical women, especially writings by the friars.

I do not categorize as melancholy those who are rationally sorry for sin, aware of their misery, and eagerly concerned about their recovery and salvation, even if it is with as great a seriousness as the faculties can bear, so long as they have sound reason, and the imagination, fantasy, or intellect is not warped or diseased. By *melancholy* I mean a diseased craziness, hurt, or error of the imagination, and consequently of the understanding. It is known by these following signs[5] (not all of which occur in every individual case of depression).

1. They are often fearful without cause, or without sufficient cause. Everything they hear or see is apt to increase their fears, especially if fear itself was the precipitant, as it often is.

2. Their imagination errs most in exaggerating their sin, danger, or unhappiness. Every peccadillo they speak of with astonishment, as if it were a heinous sin. Every possible danger they take for probable, every probable one for certain,

---

3. Baxter offers more advice in his section of *A Christian Directory* dealing with resisting despair, to which he refers the reader.

4. Jonathan Edwards deals with this definitively in *The Distinguishing Marks of a Work of the Spirit of God* (1741), included in *Jonathan Edwards on Revival* (Edinburgh: Banner of Truth, 1991).

5. Here Baxter is up to speed with modern diagnostic approaches, which emphasize the presence of some specific symptoms but rarely all the possible ones. There is wide variation among cases.

every little danger for a great one, and every calamity for an utter undoing.

3. They are consumed by excessive sadness: some cry without knowing why and even think this is somehow proper. If they should happen to smile or speak cheerfully, their consciences reproach them for it, as if they had done wrong.

4. Their religious sentiments and practices emphasize mourning and asceticism.

5. They continually accuse themselves, bringing all manner of charges against themselves, whether things they hear, read, see, or think. They second-guess themselves in everything they do, as a contentious person does with others.

6. They continuously sense themselves forsaken by God and are prone to despair. They are just like a man in a wilderness, abandoned by all his friends and comforts, despondent and disconsolate. Their continual thought is, "I am undone, undone, undone!"

7. They think that the day of grace has past and that it is now too late to repent or to find mercy. If you tell them of the tone of the gospel and its offer of free pardon to every penitent believer, they still wail, "Too late, too late, my day is past," not considering that every soul that truly repents in this life is certainly forgiven.

8. They are often tempted to look upon only the frightful aspects in the doctrine of predestination and, completely out of context, misuse them as a basis for despair. They reason that if God has rejected them (or not chosen them), all they or the whole world can do cannot save them. Next, they develop a strong conviction that they are not among the elect and are thus past help or hope. They do not understand that God does not elect anyone merely to be saved while bypassing the means. Rather, he elects in order that they will believe, repent, and thereby be saved. Election applies to both the end and the

means. All that will repent and choose Christ and a holy life are elected to salvation, because they are elected to the means and state of salvation. If they persevere, they shall enjoy salvation. To repent is the best way to prove that one is elect.

9. They never read or hear of any miserable example without identifying with it. If they hear of Cain, or of Pharaoh given up to hardness of heart, or read that some are vessels of wrath fitted to destruction or have eyes and see not, ears and hear not, hearts and understand not, they think, "This is all about me!" or, "This is just my situation." If they hear of any terrible example of God's judgments on anyone, they think it will be so with them. If anyone dies suddenly, or a house burns, or someone is delirious or dies in despair, they think it will also happen to them. The reading of Spira's[6] case causes or intensifies depression in many. The ignorant author of this case actually described a severe depression brought about by sinning against conscience. Yet, he described the case as if it were an unforgivable despair arising from a sound intellect.

10. At the same time, these persons think that no one has shared a similar plight. I have seen many very similar cases in the course of a few weeks. Yet, each one says that no one else was ever like them.[7]

---

6. See Nathaniel Bacon, *The Fearefull Estate of Francis Spira* (London, 1638). Spira was a brilliant sixteenth-century Italian lawyer who, under pressure from Roman Catholic authorities, renounced his professed evangelical convictions and subsequently believed himself damned for his action. He died from a severe melancholic depression.

7. There is such a self-preoccupation here that there is a danger of attributing to oneself the lament of Lam. 1:12:

Is it nothing to you, all you who pass by?
  Look and see
if there is any sorrow like my sorrow,
  which was brought upon me,
which the LORD inflicted
  on the day of his fierce anger.

This has been interpreted (certainly by Handel) as a Messianic prophecy. In any event, the depressed person's distorted perspective is captured by such an untintentionally profane comparison.

11. They are utterly incapable of enjoying anything. They cannot apprehend, believe, or think of anything comforting. They read all the threatenings of the Word with a ready perception and application. However, they read the promises over and over without noticing them, as if they had not read them. Or they say, "They do not belong to me: the greater the mercy of God and the riches of grace, the more miserable am I for having no part in them." They are like a man in continual pain or sickness, unable to rejoice because of the awareness of his pain. They look on husband, wife, friends, children, house, possessions, and everything else without any pleasure, like one who is going to be executed for some crime.

12. Their consciences are quick in telling them of sin and suggesting that demoralizing efforts are duties. Yet, they are oblivious to all duties that could bring consolation. As far as thanksgiving for mercies, praising God, meditating on his love and grace, and on Christ and his promises: direct them as firmly as you will; they do not see these to be their duty, nor make any conscientious effort to perform them. Rather, they think these are duties for others but unsuitable to themselves.

13. They always say that they cannot believe, and therefore think they cannot be saved. This is because they commonly misunderstand the nature of faith. They consider faith to be the belief that they themselves are forgiven and are in favor with God, and shall thus be saved. And because they cannot believe this—which their disease will not allow them to believe—they think that they are not believers. In contrast, saving faith is nothing but the belief that the gospel is true, and that Christ is the Savior to whom we trust our souls. This belief causes us to readily consent that he be ours and that we be his, and thus to agree to the covenant of grace. Yet even while they do so agree (and would give a world to be sure that Christ was theirs

and to be perfectly holy), yet they think they do not believe because they do not believe that he will forgive or save them individually.

14. They are as unhappy and discontent with themselves as a complaining, obstinate person is toward others. Think of someone hard to please, who finds fault with everything he sees or hears, is offended at everyone, and is suspicious of everybody he sees whispering. That is just how a depressed person is toward himself: suspicious, displeased, and finding fault with everything.

15. They are addicted to solitude and avoid company for the most part.

16. They are given to fixed ruminations, and long, observant thoughts that serve little purpose. Accordingly, deep musing and thinking are their primary activities and a large part of their disease.

17. They are quite averse to the work of their callings and prone to idleness, either lying in bed or sitting and thinking unprofitably by themselves.

18. They think mostly about themselves: like millstones that grind on each other in the absence of grist, so one thought brings on another. Their thoughts are *about* their thoughts. When they have been thinking strangely, they think over what they have just thought. Generally, they rarely meditate on God (unless on his wrath), heaven, Christ, the state of the church, or anything external to them. Rather, all their thoughts are constricted and turned inward. Self-torture summarizes their thoughts and lives.

19. Their perplexed thoughts are like unraveled yarn or silk, or like a man in a maze or wilderness, or one who has lost his way in the night. He is looking and groping about, and can make little of anything. He is bewildered, confused, and

entangled even more, filled with doubts and difficulties, out of which he cannot find the way.

20. His scruples are unending: he is afraid he may sin in every word he speaks, in every thought and every look, in every meal he eats, and in every article of clothes he wears. If he considers how to amend them, he has doubts over his proposed remedies. He dares neither travel nor stay at home, speak nor be silent. He obsesses about everything, as if he consisted entirely of contradictory self-doubt.

21. Accordingly, it emerges that he is highly superstitious and makes up many rules for himself that God never required of him. He traps himself with unnecessary vows and resolutions, and harmful asceticism: "touch not, taste not, handle not." His religion is so composed of such outward, self-imposed tasks[8] that he spends many hours in this or that act of supposed devotion: wearing these clothes but rejecting nicer ones, rejecting favorite foods, and many similar things. A great deal of the perfectionistic aspect of superstitious and ritualistic[9] devotion emerges from melancholy, though the ecclesiastical structure of this communion derives from pride and covetousness.

22. Such individuals have lost the power of controlling their thoughts by reason. If you convince them that they should reject their self-perplexing, unprofitable thoughts and turn their thoughts to other subjects or simply be at rest, they cannot obey you. They are under a compulsion or constraint. They cannot push out their troublesome thoughts; they cannot redirect their minds; they cannot think about love and mercy. They can think

---

8. Cf. Col. 2:18–23.

9. Baxter calls these "popish," referring to the highly ceremonial aspects that had come to be associated with Roman Catholic devotion. Baxter's antipathy to Roman Catholicism was both theological and moral, and consistent with the larger contemporary English Christian communion, both Conformist and Dissenting.

of nothing but that on which they do think, as a man with a toothache can think only of his pain.

23. They usually worsen progressively after this stage, becoming unable to engage in private prayer or meditation. Their thoughts become disordered. When they should pray or meditate, they go off on a hundred tangents, and they cannot keep their thoughts fixed on any one thing. This is the very essence of their disease: a misguided, confused imagination combined with a weakened reason that cannot control it. Sometimes terror drives them from prayer; they dare not hope and therefore dare not pray. Usually they dare not receive the Lord's Supper. Here they are most frightened. If they do receive it, they are overcome with terror, fearing that they have taken it to their own damnation by receiving it unworthily.[10]

24. Thus, they develop a powerful avoidance of all religious duty. Fear and despair cause them to approach prayer, preaching, and reading the Bible like a bear being led to the stake. They then conclude that they hate God and godliness, attributing the effects of their disease to their souls. Ironically, those of them who are godly would rather be freed from all their sins and be perfectly holy than have all the riches or honor in the world.

25. They are usually preoccupied with intense and pressured thoughts that, being so disorganized, only compete against and contradict one another. They experience this just as if something were speaking within them, and as if their own violent thoughts were the pleadings and impulses of someone else. Therefore, they tend to attribute all their fantasies to some extraordinary act of either the Devil or the Spirit of God. They express themselves in words such as these: "It was put upon my heart," or "It was said to me that I must do something. Then it was said

---

10. 1 Cor. 11:28–29.

that I must *not* do it, and I was told I must do something else!" They experience their own thoughts almost as audible voices *speaking* what they themselves are actually *thinking*.

26. When melancholy becomes intense, these individuals are frequently troubled with hideous, blasphemous temptations against God, Christ, or the Scripture, and against the immortality of the soul. This comes partly from their own fears, which make them dwell—in spite of themselves—upon what they most fear, just as blood will naturally flow from a wound. The very pain of their fears draws their thoughts to what they fear. As one who desperately longs for sleep and fears being unable to get to sleep is bound to be kept awake by those very fears and desires, so the fears and longings of the melancholy are at odds. Additionally, the malice of the Devil is plainly interfering here as well and he takes advantage by way of this disease to tempt and trouble them, and to show his hatred of God, Christ, Scripture, and them. For as he can more easily tempt a choleric person to anger, a phlegmatic, sensual person to sloth, and a sanguine or hot-tempered person to lust and immorality, so a melancholy person is more easily tempted to thoughts of blasphemy, infidelity, and despair. Often such persons feel a vehement urgency, as if inwardly compelled to speak blasphemous or foolish words. They have no rest until they yield to these impulses. Others yield to a temptation to be mute, and when they have done so are then tempted to utterly despair because they have committed so great a sin. When the Devil gets this advantage on them, he continues his efforts against them.

27. At this, they are further tempted to think they have committed the sin against the Holy Spirit, not understanding what that sin is, but still afraid of having committed it, because it is so fearful a sin. At the least they think they shall not be forgiven. They do not recognize that a temptation is one thing but a sin

another, and that no one has less cause to fear being condemned for his sin than he who is least willing in it and most hates it. No one can be less willing to commit sin than are these poor souls with respect to the hideous, blasphemous thoughts of which they complain.

28. Because of such thoughts, some of them come to think that they are demon-possessed. If it even enters their minds how possessed persons used to act, the mere power of suggestion will cause them to act the same. I have known persons that would swear, curse, blaspheme, and imitate an inward alien voice, thinking that it was the Devil in them doing it. However, few progress to this extreme.

29. Some that do experience delirium[11] hear voices and see lights and apparitions, and believe that the veil is opened before them,[12] and that someone meets them and converses with them.[13] It is, however, only the error of a malfunctioning brain and disordered imagination.[14]

30. Many of them become weary of life itself because of the constant, tiring perplexities of their minds, and yet they remain afraid of dying. Some resolutely starve themselves; others are strongly tempted to kill themselves, and are haunted with the temptation so relentlessly that they can go nowhere without feeling as if something within them goads them on and says, "Do it, do it!" Eventually, many poor souls do yield and kill themselves.

31. Many others suffer with fixed, false fears[15] of bringing want, poverty, and misery to their families, of imprisonment or

---

11. Delirium is a grave medical condition, with poor prognostic implications, and is often observed as someone is entering or emerging from a coma, or dying.

12. Referring to a parting of the barrier between this world and the next, or between the material and spiritual, the visible and invisible.

13. Near-death experiences are not newly documented phenomena.

14. Baxter offers a mundane and largely physiological explanation for these symptoms.

15. This is the actual standard clinical definition of *delusion*.

banishment, or that somebody will kill them. They believe that anyone they see whispering is plotting to murder them.[16]

32. Some determine not to speak a word, and so they remain a long time in resolute silence.

33. All of them are intractable and stubborn in their opinions, and cannot be talked out of them, no matter how irrational.

34. Few of them respond positively to any reason, persuasion, or counsel. If it does seem to satisfy, quiet, and cheer them for the moment, the next day they are just as bad as before. It is the nature of their illness to think the way they do.[17] Their thoughts are not cured, because the underlying disease itself remains uncured.

35. Yet in all this distress, few of them will believe that they are depressed, and they hate being told that they are. They insist it is merely a rational sense of unhappiness from being forsaken and under the heavy wrath of God. Therefore, they can hardly be persuaded to take any medication or use other means for the cure of their bodies. They maintain that they are well, being confident that it is only their souls that are distressed.

This is the miserable case of these unfortunate people, greatly to be pitied and not to be despised by anyone. I have spoken here only what I myself have frequently observed and known. Let no one look down on these individuals; persons of all sorts fall into this misery: educated and illiterate, high and low, good and bad, as well as some who previously lived in decadent self-seeking and sensuality until God made them aware of their foolishness.

The causes of melancholy are (1) most commonly some temporal loss, suffering, grief, or worry that has affected them too deeply; (2) an excessive fear of common if nevertheless dangerous

---

16. This represents a dangerous example of what is termed a paranoid delusional state.
17. It is notable that Baxter refuses to "blame the victim" but instead takes a very compassionate and understanding posture.

situations; (3) too strenuous and unremitting intellectual work or thought, which has confused and strained the imagination too intensely; (4) fears, too deep or too constant, and serious, passionate thoughts and cares about the danger of the soul.[18] (5) The major predispositions to it (indeed the principal causes) are a frailness of faculty and reason, joined with strong emotions (most often found in women and those who otherwise come by them naturally). (6) Finally, in some cases, melancholy is ushered in by some heinous sin, the sight of which those guilty of it cannot bear, once their consciences are finally awakened.

When the natural course of this disease is far advanced, counsel to the affected persons themselves is useless, because they have no rationality or free will to implement it. Rather, it is their friends nearest them that need counsel.[19] But at least initially, *most* persons continue to retain some power of reason, so I give instructions here for *their* benefit.

*Direction 1.*[20] Be sure that a theological error is not the root of your distress. Especially have a solid understanding of the covenant of grace and the riches of mercy revealed in Christ. It will be useful to you to understand these following truths, among others.

1. Our thoughts of the infinite goodness of God should be proportionate to our thoughts concerning his infinite power and wisdom.

2. The mercy of God has provided for all mankind so sufficient a Savior that no sinner shall perish for lack of a complete satisfaction made for his sins by Christ. No man's salvation or pardon requires that he provide satisfaction for his own sins.

---

18. Concern about the state of one's soul today is conspicuous by its general absence.

19. The necessity of family involvement in the treatment of and recovery from severe psychiatric disorders has long been an accepted standard of care.

20. Having extensively *described* melancholy, Baxter now *applies* this knowledge by telling how to deal with depression.

3. Christ has in his gospel covenant (which is an act of self-sacrifice) given himself with pardon and salvation to all that will penitently and believingly accept the offer. None perish that hear the gospel but the final, obstinate refusers of Christ and life.

4. He who believes the truth of the gospel so far as to consent to the covenant of grace—that God the Father would be his Lord and reconciled Father, and Christ his Savior, and the Holy Spirit his sanctifier—has true, saving faith and a right to the blessing of the covenant.

5. The day of grace is so coextensive or equal to our lifetime that whoever truly repents and consents to the covenant of grace before his death is certainly pardoned and in a state of life. It is everyone's duty to do so, that pardon may be had.

6. Satan's temptations are not our sins: it is only our yielding to temptation that is sin.

7. The effects of natural sickness or disease are not (in and of themselves) sins.

8. The smallest sins (formally) and least likely to condemn us are those which we are most unwilling to commit and least love or enjoy.

9. No sin that we hate more than we love shall condemn us, if we would rather leave and be delivered from it than keep it. This is true repentance.

10. He is truly sanctified who would rather be perfect in holiness of heart and life, in loving God, and in living by faith than to have the greatest pleasures, riches, or honors of the world, considering also the means by which both are attained.

11. He who has this grace and desire may know that he is elect. Making our calling sure by consenting to the holy covenant is also how we make our election sure.[21]

---

21. 2 Pet. 1:10.

12. The same thing that is a great duty to some may be no duty at all to another who, because of physical illness (fevers, delirium, melancholy, etc.), is unable to do it.[22]

*Direction 2.* Be careful about worldly concerns, sorrow, and discontentment. Do not treasure earthly things so much that you let them upset you. Instead, learn to cast your cares on God. You will find less peace in any suffering that comes about through such a worldly, sinful means. It is much safer to be distracted by cares for heaven than by cares for this world.[23]

*Direction 3.* Meditation is not a duty at all for a melancholy person, except for the few that are able to tolerate a brief, structured sort of meditation. This must be on something furthest from the matter that troubles them, except for short meditations like sudden, spontaneous prayers said out loud. A rigid and protracted meditation will only frustrate and disturb you, and render you unable to perform other duties. If a man has a broken leg, he must not walk on it until it is set, or the whole body will suffer. It is your thinking faculty or your imagination that is the broken, hurting part. Therefore, you must not use it to reflect upon the things that so trouble you. Perhaps you will say, "That is profane, neglects God and the soul, and lets the Tempter have his will!" But I answer, "No, it is simply to refrain from what you cannot presently do, so that by doing other things that you can, you may later do what you cannot do now. It is merely to postpone attempting what (at present) will

---

22. This is the principle of diminished responsibility, a long-established legal precedent.

23. The Puritans conceptualized our journey from this life (a.k.a. "The City of Destruction," per John Bunyan) to heaven ("The Celestial City," also Bunyan) as a dangerous one along an often treacherous path, beset by many obstacles, enemies, and snares. This path demands courage (the golden mean between despair and rashness) along with the other classical and Christian virtues. Here Baxter admonishes us to exercise prudence or discretion.

only make you less able to do all your other duties. At present, you are able to conduct the affairs of your soul by sanctified reasoning. I am not dissuading you from repenting or believing, but rather from fixed, long, and deep meditations that will only hurt you."

*Direction 4.* Do not engage too long a time in any private duty you find yourself unable to bear. Prayer itself, when you are all but incapable of it, must be performed only to the degree that you are able. When you are unable to do better, then short confessions and requests to God will have to serve rather than lengthy private prayers.[24] If sickness may excuse a man for being curt because strength is low, then the same principle applies here in a sickness of the brain and spirits. God has not ordained for you to engage in activities that are harmful to you.

*Direction 5.* Where you find yourselves incapable of private devotions, don't be too hard on yourselves. Instead, go at a pace that is not too uncomfortable. Why? Because every effort that does not enable you only hinders you, makes duty wearisome to you, and further disables you by worsening your condition. It is like an ox that pulls unevenly or a horse that chafes at the bit and is thus quickly exhausted. Preserve your willingness to fulfill your duty, and avoid things that make it miserable for you. When your stomach is upset, it is not eating a lot but digesting well that restores health. Little must be eaten when much cannot be digested; so too in the case of your meditations and private devotions.

*Direction 6.* Spend the most effort on duties you are best able to tolerate. For most, this will consist of praying out loud,

---

24. Compare Paul's words in 2 Cor. 8:12: "For if the readiness is there, it is acceptable according to what a person has, not according to what he does not have."

in the presence of others, and good conversation. A sick man whose stomach cannot tolerate most foods must eat what he can tolerate. And God has provided a variety of means so that one may be effective when the others are not. Do not misunderstand me: in matters of absolute necessity—let me emphasize—you must endeavor to do them no matter what.[25] If you are slow to believe, to repent, to love God and your neighbor, to be sober, righteous, and godly, or even to pray at all, then here you must strive and not excuse yourself because of reluctance. These duties must be done, or you are lost.[26] But someone who cannot read may be saved without reading, and someone in prison or sickness may be saved without hearing the Word preached and without the communion of saints. In the same way, a person disabled by melancholy may be saved by brief reflections and quick prayers without formal and lengthy meditations and solitary prayer. Other duties that he is able to do will make up for the lack of these. Just as nature has provided two eyes, two ears, two nostrils, two kidneys, and two lungs so that if one fails the other may compensate, so it is here.

*Direction 7.* Avoid all unnecessary solitude and, as much as possible, keep honest, cheerful company. You need others and are not sufficient unto yourselves. God will use and honor others as extensions of his hands to deliver his blessings. Solitude is for those who are fit for it and provides an excellent time for meditation and conversation with God and with our

---

25. As noted earlier (p. 65), Paul says in Gal. 6:2, 5: "Bear one another's burdens, and so fulfill the law of Christ. . . . For each will have to bear his own load." While superficially paradoxical, the text suggests that some loads are overwhelming and cannot possibly be withstood alone, and that those who are able should help those who are in danger of being crushed by such weight. At the same time, there are personal responsibilities—loads—that fall to, and only to, the individual. These must not be neglected and cannot be delegated to or assumed by another.

26. Baxter is not suggesting that we are saved *by* our making diligent use of means of grace, but he is saying that we are not saved *without* making use of them, either.

own hearts. But for you, it is a time of temptation and danger. If Satan tempted Christ himself when he was fasting and alone in a wilderness, how much more will he take this as his opportunity against you? Solitude invites pondering and reflection, which are the things you must escape if you would not lose everything.

*Direction 8.* When blasphemous or disturbing thoughts intrude, or fruitless reflections, confront them immediately, and use the authority of reason that remains with you to reject them and command them to depart. If you have not lost your reason, it and your will have power over the thoughts as well as over the tongue, hands, or feet. Just as you would be ashamed to run in circles or fight with your fists and then say, "I cannot help it," or to let yourself talk incessantly all day and say, "I cannot stop it," so should you be ashamed to let your thoughts continue randomly, or upon hurtful things, and then say, "I cannot help it." Are you doing the best you can to help it? Can you not turn your thoughts to something else? Or can you not rouse yourself and shake them off? Some individuals, by splashing a little cold water in their faces (or by asking someone to do it for them),[27] can arouse themselves from melancholic torpor as if from sleep. If not this, can you not get out of your room and begin some task that will serve as a diversion? You might do more than you have done if you were just willing and knew how much it is your responsibility to do so.

*Direction 9.* When you do think of holy things, let it be of the best things: of God and grace, Christ, heaven, or your

---

27. Note the initiative is with the depressed individual to self-administer this treatment or to request it. It is *not* to be imagined that slapping someone or throwing water in a person's face unbidden is being advocated, as in some of the ridiculous "cures" of hysteria portrayed in older motion pictures. In such parody, the individual can always be counted on to respond with a grateful, "Thanks, I needed that." This is *not* Baxter's method.

brethren or the church. Focus your meditations outwardly, but be sure you do not examine yourself in detail, and don't waste your thoughts thinking *about* your thoughts. Just as we need to direct the thoughts of careless sinners inwardly and turn them from the world and sin and to themselves, in a different way we need to direct the thoughts of self-perplexing, melancholy persons outwardly. This is so because it is the nature of their disorder to be always accusing themselves. Remember that it is a far higher, nobler, and sweeter work to think of God, Christ, and heaven, than of such worms as we ourselves are. When we go to God, we go to love and light and liberty. When we look down into ourselves, we look into a dungeon, a prison, a wilderness, a place of darkness, horror, filthiness, misery, and confusion. Therefore, though such thoughts are necessary, in that without them our repentance and due watchfulness cannot be maintained, yet they are grievous, ignoble, and even fruitless in comparison with our thoughts of God. When you pore over the contents of your heart to search whether or not the love of God is there, it would be wiser to think of the infinite friendliness of God. That will stir up love of God, whether or not it was there before. So instead of trying so hard to read your heart to know whether or not it is fixed upon heaven, *lift up your thoughts to heaven* and think of its glory. That will raise your heart heavenward and give you and show you what you were searching for. Devote time to plant holy desires in the garden of your heart, time that you presently spend probing and examining yourself while hoping to discern if those desires are there. We are such darkened, confused creatures that the sight of ourselves is enough to provoke loathing and a horror in our minds, and to contribute to melancholy. But in God and glory there is nothing to discourage our thoughts and everything to delight them if Satan does not manage to misrepresent him to us.

*Direction 10.* Do not overlook the miracle of love that God has shown us in the wonderful incarnation, office, life, death, resurrection, ascension, and reign of our Redeemer. Rather, steep your thoughts most of all in these wonders of mercy, ordained by God to be the primary substance of your thoughts. You should rationally bring to mind many thoughts about Christ and grace for each one you list about your sin and misery. God requires you to see your sin and misery, but in a manner that tends to magnify the remedy and to cause you to embrace it. Never think of sin and hell alone, but as the way to thoughts of Christ and grace. This is the duty of even the worst of us. Are your sins ever before you?[28] Why not also the pardoning grace in Christ?[29] Is hell open before you? Why is not the Redeemer also before you? Do you say, "Because sin and hell are mine, but Christ, holiness, and heaven are not mine"? Then I answer you, "It is so because you want it that way: if you would not have it that way, then it *is not* that way." God has set life first before you, and not only death. He has put Christ, holiness, and heaven on his side of the scales; the Devil puts the pleasure of sin for a season on the other. The one you choose without any pretense *is* yours. God has given you your choice. Nothing is more true than this: God has so fully given Christ and life to all who hear the gospel that nothing but their final obstinate refusal can condemn them.[30] Christ and life are brought to the will and choice of everyone, though not everyone will accept and choose him. So if you would not have Christ, life, and holiness, what would you rather have? And if not, what are you complaining about?[31]

---

28. Ps. 51:3.
29. So much for the doom-and-gloom caricature of the Puritans!
30. John 3:16; 5:40; 1 John 5:10–12; Rev. 22:17.
31. The use of paradox in counseling is not a modern innovation.

*Direction 11.* Think and speak as much about the mercy you have received as you do about the sin you have committed. Similarly, focus as much on the mercy offered as on the mercy you need. You dare not say that the mercy you have received is less worthy to be remembered and mentioned than are all your sins. When God does so much for you, should it be overlooked, glossed over, and dismissed as if his mercies were a bare bone or a barren wilderness that would yield no food for thought? Do not be guilty of such great ingratitude. Thoughts of love and mercy would breed love and sweetness in the soul. By contrast, thoughts of sin and wrath only breed indisposition, terror, bitterness, and perplexity. These latter drive the heart away from God.

*Direction 12.* Commit yourself daily to spending as great a part of your prayers in confessing mercy received as in confessing sin committed, and in praising God as in lamenting your own miseries. You dare not deny this to be your duty, if indeed you comprehend your duty. Thanksgiving and praise are greater duties than confessing sin and misery. Resolve then that they shall have the largest share of time. If you will simply do this much—which you can do if you will—it will in time remove the bitterness of your spirit. The very frequent mention of sweeter things will sweeten your mind and change your temperament and habit, as change of diet affects the vigor of the body. I implore you: be resolved and try this approach. If you cannot mention mercy as thankfully as you would like or mention God's excellencies with the degree of devotion and praise as you would, nevertheless do what you can and mention them as you *are* able.[32] You may apportion your time, deciding what shall have the greatest portion in prayer, even if you

---

32. We are here admonished not to let what we truly *cannot* do serve as an excuse for neglecting what we *can* do.

cannot control your feelings. You will find very great benefit, if only you will do this.

*Direction 13.* Do not value too highly the passionate aspect of duty, but understand this: judgment, will, practice, high esteem of God and holiness, resolute choice, and sincere endeavor are the life of grace and duty; felt emotions are lesser and uncertain things. You don't know what you do when you so emphasize the emotional aspect, or when you strive so much for deep and transcendent revelations. These are not the important things or the essentials of holiness. Too much of such feelings may distract you. God knows how much you are able to bear. Passionate feelings depend considerably upon nature. Some persons are more expressive than others. A little thing affects some deeply. The wisest and most worthy persons are usually the least passionate. The weakest hardly control their feelings.[33] God is not apprehended by our senses, and therefore is better experienced through the understanding and will than through the emotions. The holiest soul is the one most inclined toward God, resolved for him, and conformed to his will, not the one affected with the deepest griefs, and fears, and joys, and other such transporting emotions. Nevertheless, it would be best if holy affections could be stirred up at will, to a degree that would best equip us for duty. But I have known many who complain for lack of deeper feelings, who if their feelings (as they call their emotions) had been more intense, might have been distracted. I would rather be a Christian who loathes himself for sin, resolves against it, and forsakes it (though he cannot cry over it) than one of those who can weep today but sin again tomorrow, one whose sinful emotions are as quickly stirred as his better ones.

---

33. I believe Baxter is here arguing for self-control, not absence of expressed emotion.

*Direction 14.* Don't be too preoccupied with your own thoughts. Do not take not too much notice of them. If Satan tosses in abusive thoughts, and if you are unable to cast them out, make light of them, and take less notice of them. Making a great deal of every thought that enters your mind will keep those thoughts in your mind longer. For what we are most aware of we think most about. What we least regard we least remember. If you want never to get rid of them, then keep paying attention to them and making too great a matter of them. These troublesome thoughts are like bothersome harpies: if you incline to them and answer them, they will never leave you alone. If you let them talk, take no notice of them, and make no answer to them, they will be weary and give up. The Devil's design is to annoy and unsettle you. If he sees that you will not be bothered and unsettled, he will give up.[34] I already know your response: "Should I be so ungodly as to make light of such sinful thoughts?" I am advising you not to make so light of them as to be unconcerned what thoughts are in your mind or to dismiss a small sin as if it were not one. But do not take them for greater or more dangerous sins than they really are.[35] Do not take distinct, particular notice of them or disturb yourselves about them. If you do, you will have no room in your thoughts for Christ and heaven and what *should* take up your thoughts. Instead, the Devil will rejoice to see how he occupies you in thinking your own thoughts after yourself[36] (or rather his temptations). He can busy you all day in listening to what he will say to you and thinking of his suggestions instead of the works of God. None of God's servants are free of inconsistent and sinful thoughts. For such thoughts, they must ask for daily

---

34. James 4:7.

35. 1 John 5:16–17 states clearly that some sins are worse than others. Baxter here counsels against dismissing any sin as "insignificant" because it is "small," or elevating it above the grace of Christ because it is "huge."

36. We are rather to "think God's thoughts after him."

forgiveness and rejoice that they have a sufficient Savior and remedy for them, and that, accordingly, sin will finally lead only to the exalting of grace. But if they should excessively attend to and be troubled by every groundless thought, it would merely be a snare to divert them from almost all their greater duties. Would you like it if your employee began noticing and worrying about insignificant imperfections in his work instead of *doing* his work?

*Direction 15.* Remember, it is no sin to be tempted, but only to yield to the temptation. Christ himself was carried about and tempted blasphemously by the Devil—tempted even to fall down and worship him. Yet Christ turned these temptations to an advantage, increasing his glory through his victory over them. Don't think that the Devil's sin is yours. Are your temptations more horrid and odious than Christ's were? What if the Devil had carried you to the pinnacle of the temple as he did Christ? Would you not have thought that God had forsaken you and given you up to the power of Satan? You may reason that you yield to temptation while Christ did not. Well, it cannot be expected that sinful people should bear temptation as innocently as Christ did, can it? Satan found nothing in Christ to conform to him, but in us he finds a sinful nature! Wax will receive an impression, whereas marble will not. But not every sinful taint represents consent to the sin that tempts us.

*Direction 16.* Consider how far you are from loving, delighting in, or being reluctant to leave these sinful thoughts. Note that no sin condemns except sin that is so loved and delighted in that you would rather keep it than leave it.[37] Do you not long to be delivered from all these horrid thoughts

---

37. The Puritans would necessarily be more concerned with causes than with consequences. So one who fears and hates the cause of final condemnation (sin) has less to fear than one who merely fears the consequences (hell).

and sins? Would you be unwilling to live in disgrace, poverty, or exile if you might only be free from sin? If so, why doubt the pardon of it? Can you have any surer sign of repentance or that your sin is not a ruling, unpardoned sin than the fact that you do *not* love and desire it? The less willingness to sin, the less sin; and the more willingness to sin, the more sin. The covetous man loves his money, the fornicator loves his lust, the proud man loves his honor, the drunkard loves his drinks, and the glutton loves to indulge his appetite. They so love these that they will not leave them. But do you love your disturbing, confused, or blasphemous thoughts? Are you not so weary of them as to be even weary of your lives because of them? Would you not be glad and grateful to be never troubled with them again? So how can you doubt being forgiven them?

*Direction 17.* Don't blame yourself any more than there is cause to do for the effects of your disease. Indirectly, a man who in his distraction thinks or speaks inappropriately may be said to be at fault *to the degree that his sin has caused his illness.* But directly and in and of itself, *the involuntary effects of sickness are not sinful.* Depression is simply a disease affecting the emotions and imagination, though you sense no illness. It is as expected for a depressed person to be impetuous and tormented with doubts, fears, despairing thoughts, and blasphemous temptations as it is for a man to talk incoherently in a fever when his cognition fails. Similarly, how common it is for a fever to provoke thoughts of water and powerful thirst. Would you have a man in a fever accuse himself for being thirsty or for such thoughts, desire, or talk? If you had the hideous thoughts in your dreams that you now have while awake, would you not classify them as unavoidable weaknesses rather than unpardoned sins? Accordingly, your disorder makes your evil thoughts morally equivalent to dreams.

*Direction 18.* Be sure that you keep yourself constantly busy—as far as your strength will allow—in the diligent labors of a lawful calling,[38] and don't waste precious time in idleness. Idleness is the opportunity of the Tempter: when you are idle, you invite the Devil to come and annoy you. Then you will have time to listen to him and think about all that he will put into your mind, and then to think those thoughts again![39] When you have nothing else to do, the Devil will find you this kind of work. Then you will have to sit still and muse, and your thoughts will of necessity be stirring in the muddle of your own distemper, as children playing in the mud. And *idleness is a sin,* which God will not countenance. He has commanded you, "Six days you shall labor."[40] And,

> By the sweat of your face
> you shall eat bread.[41]

And, "If anyone is not willing to work, let him not eat."[42] Remember that time is precious, and flies away, and God has given you none without a purpose. Therefore, as you are troubled for other sins, make this sin a matter of conscience, and do not waste even a quarter of an hour in idle, unprofitable musings. It would be fitting were God to make your sin itself to be your punishment, and your own idle thoughts to chastise you daily, if you will not get up and go about your lawful business. No pretense of prayer or any devotion will excuse your idleness, for it is against the law of God. Above all that I have said to you, let me entreat you therefore to obey this one direction.

---

38. The concept of a vocational calling is wonderfully addressed by Paul Helm, *The Callings: The Gospel in the World* (Carlisle, PA: Banner of Truth, 1987).

39. If we do not think "God's thoughts after him," we will first think our own thoughts over and over, and eventually come to think the Devil's thoughts after him, so Baxter seems to be saying.

40. Ex. 20:9, the fourth commandment.

41. Gen. 3:19.

42. 2 Thess. 3:10.

I have known despairing, melancholy persons cured by setting themselves resolutely and diligently about their duties (and changing locations and company, and going outside.) If you insist on brooding in a corner and sin against God through idleness and wasting time, and thus contribute to your own misery rather than rouse yourself to go about your business, then your tragedy is well deserved. Don't say that you have little or nothing to do. God has made it everyone's duty, no matter how rich, to labor in such employment as is suitable to one's position and ability.

*Direction 19.* Note carefully how much the Devil delights in confining you to sad, despondent thoughts. You may then easily see that such a focus cannot be your duty or in your best interests if it is so helpful and pleasing to the Devil! By keeping you in self-perplexing doubts and fears, he robs God of the thanks and praise you owe him for all his mercies. These highest duties you cast aside, as if they did not belong to you. You fail to give God the honor of his most miraculous mercy in our redemption; nor do you study, relish, admire, or magnify the riches of grace in Jesus Christ! You have poor, low thoughts of the infinite love of God and are unfit to weigh it or perceive it. You are like someone with constant acid reflux, which causes a continual bitterness in the mouth and hinders one from taking any enjoyment in eating. Your low thoughts of God prevent you from loving him and incline you to hate him or to flee from him as from an enemy. Meanwhile, the Devil misrepresents him as hating you. This wastes your time; it deprives you of all readiness and pleasure in duty, and turns all God's service into burden and bother. It is very contrary to the spirit of adoption, and to the whole frame of evangelical worship and obedience. And will you—under pretense of being more humble, sorrowful, and insightful—thus gratify Satan and wrong God and yourselves?[43]

*Direction 20.* Do not trust your own judgment in your depressed and anxious condition, as to either the state of your soul or the choice and conduct of your thoughts or ways. Commit yourself to the judgment and direction of some experienced, faithful guide. In this dark, disordered condition, you are unfit to judge your own condition or the way to approach your duty. Your mind and imagination are either well or sick: if they are well, then what are these complaints about disturbances, confusion, and an inability to meditate and pray? If they are sick, then why will you be so conceited as to think yourself able to evaluate yourself while having such a disturbed imagination and thinking? One of the worst characteristics of depressed persons is that they are often wise in their own eyes and stubborn in their own opinions at a time when their brains are sickest and their reason weakest. Further, they are smug, headstrong, and unteachable, as if they are proud of their pitiful understanding and think nobody knows so much as they.[44] "Oh!" they say, "you don't understand my case!" Am I not more likely to understand your case for having seen so many others like it than are you who never experienced depression in anyone but yourself? An observant bystander may better understand the situation of someone who is dreaming than the dreamer can understand his own situation. You say that others do not feel what you feel! Well, no more does a physician feel

---

43. Obsessive perfectionism can represent the most arrogant form of self-righteousness. While superficially self-abnegating, it is pride masquerading as humility. Idiomatically, we refer to such an attitude as "being more Catholic than the pope." Baxter argues that such perfectionism is so far from being a higher state of grace as to be actual sin.

44. It is impossible to learn anything if you know everything.

what someone with a fever or epilepsy or delirium feels. Yet, on the basis of what you say you feel and what he sees, he far better understands your disorder—both the nature and the cure of it—than you who feel it. A wise person, when sick, will entrust himself, under God, to the direction of his physician and the help of his friends, and not resist their help and advice or willfully refuse it just because it doesn't please him. Do the same, if you are wise. Trust yourself to some appropriate advice. Don't despise the giver's judgment about either your condition or your duty. You think that you are lost and that there is no hope. Listen to someone in a better position to judge. Don't set your limited understanding too obstinately against him. Do you think he is so foolish as to be mistaken? Should not humility instead cause you to consider that *you* may be mistaken? Accept his advice about your thoughts, the manner and length of your private devotions, and all your misgivings for which you need advice. Answer me this one question: Do you know anyone who is wiser than you and more able to evaluate your condition and advise you? If you say no, then how proud you are of such a crazed wit! If you say yes, then believe and trust that person, and resolve to follow his direction. And I would ask you, did you not once hold a very different opinion about yourself? If so, were you not then as sound of mind and as able to judge, and more likely to be right, than you are now?

*Direction 21.* My last advice is this: strive for the cure of your disease, and commit yourself to the care of your physician and obey him. Don't be like most depressed persons, who will not believe that medication will do them good, but who think it is only their soul that is troubled. Because—understand this—it is the chemistry, reason, and mood that are unbalanced. Accordingly, the soul is like someone who looks through colored glass and thinks everything is the same color as the glass. I have personally known many individuals to be cured by medication.[45] What is more, unless the body is cured, the mind will hardly ever be cured,[46] so that even the most lucid and well-reasoned advice will prove ineffective.[47]

---

45. Many of the medications to which Baxter likely refers would be considered *poisons* today, in that the side-effects of such medications ("physic") were often much more pronounced than any purported therapeutic effects. Nevertheless, Baxter would have been, as a lay physician and the *only* medical expert for his congregation, familiar with the pharmacopoeia of his day. His testimony ("I have personally known many individuals to be cured by medication") we must take at face value, as he does not appear to be making claims as nearly universal as those which have been falsely made for certain modern medications. But it is reasonable to infer that if the crude medications of Baxter's day—which included things like mercurials and arsenicals—proved at times effective, we might consider our modern pharmacological offerings at least as useful.

46. Baxter is arguing not for the preeminence of the body over the mind but for the *necessity* of the body, that the mind may exist and function normally. As the brain is integral to the working of the body, so that portion of the body is particularly essential to the working of the mind.

47. There are times when advice, counseling, or formal psychotherapy alone suffice to treat both anxiety and depression. However, there are times when these methods are ineffective without medication and can be worse than ineffective unless accompanied by proper medical care.

*Chapter 4*

# THE RESOLUTION OF DEPRESSION AND OVERWHELMING GRIEF THROUGH FAITH

Richard Baxter[1]

Question: What are the best protections against depression and overwhelming sorrow?

"... or he may be overwhelmed by excessive sorrow."
(2 Cor. 2:7)

Since the brevity of my presentation does not give me the liberty, I cannot spend time developing the context of this verse or speculate on whether the person of whom it speaks is the

---

1. Edited and updated by Michael S. Lundy, MD, from Baxter's original "The Cure of Melancholy and Overmuch Sorrow, by Faith."

same individual indicted and judged for incest in 1 Corinthians 5 or is someone else. Similarly, I decline to take up the argument by one expositor who believes that the condemned man was actually a bishop of the church in Achaia, and that a formal gathering of his fellow bishops was responsible for his excommunication. Further, the additional speculation regarding opinions as to the proportional representation of each congregation by a specific bishop is irrelevant here. So also are the discussions regarding the question of schism if the individual cited were a bishop and, upon his excommunication (demanded by Paul), managed to retain a following that rejected the excommunication, and so on. The only portion of this verse that is relevant to my present concern is the last sentence, which provides the reason that the censured offender, who has expressed sincere repentance, should be forgiven and restored: "or he may be overwhelmed by excessive sorrow."

This last sentence expresses three practical matters of doctrine, each intimately related to the other two, which I will address as a whole. Specifically, these are the points:

1. Sorrow and grief, even for actual and heinous sin, may be excessive.
2. Excessive sorrow will devour a person.
3. Accordingly, such sorrow must be resisted and assuaged by appropriate comfort from others, but which should also come from within our own souls.

These concerns will be addressed in this manner and in the following order:

1. What actually represents excessive sorrow
2. The means by which this sort of sorrow devours and destroys one

3. The causes of such sorrow
4. The effective resolution of such sorrow

———

It should go without saying that excessive sorrow for real sin is hardly a common state of affairs in this world. Rather, a willfully ignorant and stubborn disposition is the common cause of people's perdition. The ubiquity of a hard heart and an insensitive conscience protects most people from a proper sense of the gravity of their sin, or at least from an awareness of the danger, misery, and eternal ramifications for their guilty souls. A languorous familiarity with sin deprives most individuals of awareness or comprehension. They may perform some of the external acts of religion, but as if in a dream: they attend church; they repeat the words of the creed, the Lord's Prayer, and the liturgical recitation of the Ten Commandments; and they even receive Communion, but as if asleep to the implications of them all. While they agree that sin is the most hateful thing in God's sight and hurtful to their fellow men (and women), they nevertheless live in sin with delight and obstinacy. They imagine themselves to repent of it, but when they are not persuaded to actually forsake it, they instead direct their own hatred to those who would encourage them to make a clean break from sin.

Such individuals will not see themselves to be either as evil or as unbalanced as those who experience an effective sorrow for past sins or their present unrighteous state, or who make solid resolutions to live a new and holy life. Instead they dream, so to speak, of judgment, heaven, and hell, yet their reactions to these last things are not consonant with the unbearable weightiness of them.[2] Would they not be more concerned about them were they

———

2. See Paul Helm, *The Last Things: Death, Judgment, Heaven and Hell* (Carlisle, PA: Banner of Truth, 1989).

spiritually awake to these matters? They think of, listen to, and even discuss the great work of man's redemption by Christ, and of the need of justifying and sanctifying grace, and of the joys and miseries of the life to come in a manner that is thoroughly flippant and disengaged. Yet they state that they believe these things! When we preach or speak with them of the most important things—the eternal verities—citing the best evidence and in the plainest and most earnest words, it is as if speaking to the dead or to those sound asleep. While they have ears, they don't actually hear, and nothing affects their hearts.

It may be supposed that those who read the Bible and profess a belief in both its promise of eternal glory and its threat of eternal and dreadful punishment would be acutely aware of certain matters. Namely, one expects them to see the need for holiness to receive the aforementioned promise, and for a Savior to deliver them from their sin and its punishment: hell. The certainty of passing into that unseen world and the nearness anyone of us may be to such a passage at any moment should produce an energetic and enduring effort to moderate such dangers and to carry the otherwise unbearable weight of these things. However, this is not the case for most, who have such little regard for such matters—or at least have no sense of their gravity—that they find neither time on their schedules nor room in their hearts for them. Instead, they hear of them as they might of some foreign land in which they have no personal interest and no thought of ever visiting. Their casual refusal to prepare for the inevitable and their focus on this present world and their lives in it suggest them to be joking[3] or half-awake when they do admit that they will someday themselves die. When their own friends die and are buried, and they stare at the

---

3. Cf. Gen. 19:14: "So Lot went out and said to his sons-in-law, who were to marry his daughters, 'Up! Get out of this place, for the LORD is about to destroy the city.' But he seemed to his sons-in-law to be jesting."

stark evidence of death, they themselves behave as if in a dream, as if their own deaths could not possibly be near. If we knew how to wake up such sinners, they would come to themselves, as it were, and think very differently about such weighty matters. Their serious turn of mind would be quickly manifested by a very different kind of life. Nevertheless, God will eventually wake everyone up—including those now least inclined to it—through either grace or punishment.

It is exactly because a hard heart constitutes so much of the error and misery of the unconverted, and because a soft and tender heart is so integral to the new nature as promised by Christ, that some who are newly converted imagine that they can never overdo their newfound sorrow for sin. Rather, they so fear being hard-hearted that they end up being nearly swallowed alive by an excessive, exaggerated sorrow. Even though this excessive sorrow may be for real sins, past or present, it is a dangerous virtue, as it were, and as such, none at all. To wear such excessive sorrow as a badge of honor or as an evidence of duty, or to fail to understand the danger in such a misguided attitude, leads to further mistakes. Some have imagined that only those Christians who are most doubtful, fearful, and sorrowful—and most likely to be morose and constant complainers—are truly sincere in faith. This represents a serious error.

## When Is Sorrow Excessive?

1. Sorrow is excessive when it arises from false premises. Any sorrow is excessive if none at all is appropriate, and a great sorrow is excessive if it is disproportionate to the actual cause. If one believes it to be a matter of duty to accomplish what is no duty at all, but feels guilty for having left the matter undone, this is guilt caused by error. Many have felt very guilty because they found themselves unable to pray with sufficient fervor or

for what they deemed a sufficient duration, for which they possessed neither the ability nor the time. Others have felt guilty for not pointing out sin in another, when the actual need was for wise instruction and carefully worded intimation rather than formal rebuke. More become obsessed with a sense of sin when, during their workday, they think of "unspiritual" things necessary to their business rather than about God.

These guilty sensations follow from superstition, when individuals have placed upon themselves religious duties that God never required of them, and they have fallen short in performing these self-imposed obligations. Others have, falsely, become convinced that what they once held as true doctrine might be false, and then are confused and imagine that they are obligated to renounce as false what they have long held to be true. Some become preoccupied with every bit of food they eat, what they wear, and what they say. Accordingly, they develop an inverted sense of good and evil, think the good they do is sinful, and exaggerate unavoidable minor imperfections as heinous crimes. These represent examples of pain and guilt that have no valid cause and are therefore exaggerated.

2. Guilt is excessive when it is self-destructive in either a physical or an intellectual sense. Nature requires being taken seriously, and its enjoyment requires a proper exercise of duties attached to healthy living. But clearly, such gravity and associated duties must not alone or together be understood or implemented in a way that is harmful to one's own well-being. Just as civil, church, and family laws are intended in each realm for building up and not for their destruction, so also personal discipline is for one's good, not harm. As God has stated his preference for mercy over sacrifice, it is clear that we are not to use religion as a pretense to do harm to ourselves or our neighbors. We are told to love our neighbors as we do ourselves. Fasting, for example, may be considered a duty only so far as

it advances a specified good (such as expressing humility or gaining control of a particular temptation). Likewise, sorrow is excessive when it does more harm than good. But more on this specific matter later.

## How Excessive Sorrow Overcomes a Person

When sorrow overwhelms someone who is aware of being a sinner, it is overdone and needs to be subdued, as in the following examples.

1. A person's mental faculties may be diminished because of grief and trouble, so that judgment is corrupted and perverted, and therefore not to be trusted. Similarly, like someone in a rage, one in great fear and perplexity thinks of things not as they actually are but as his distraught emotional state presents them to him. In matters of God and religion, the state of his own soul and his behavior, or his own friends or enemies, his judgment is untrustworthy because it is impaired. If it can be trusted at all, it can be trusted to be more likely false than accurate. It is rather like having seriously inflamed eyes and yet thinking that what is seen through those eyes represents the true state of things. So when reason is overcome by sorrow, then sorrow itself is overdone.

2. Excessive grief prevents one from being able to govern his own thoughts. Such thoughts are guaranteed to be both sinful and distressing. Grief carries such thoughts along as if in a torrent. It would be easier to keep leaves on a tree motionless during a windstorm than to bring about calm thoughts in those who are so disturbed. If one employs reason in an effort to keep them away from agonizing subjects or to direct them to more pleasant matters, it proves fruitless. Reason alone is powerless against such a stream of violent emotions.

3. Such overwhelming sorrow would engulf faith itself and strongly prevents its exercise. The gospel asks us to believe

things that consist of unspeakable joy; it is with great difficulty that a heart overwhelmed by sorrow could believe that anything joyful is true, much less to believe things as truly joyful as pardon and salvation. While not quite daring to call God a liar, the person so overwhelmed has a hard time believing God's promises to be freely given and abundant, or that God is ready to receive all sinners who repent and return to him. Such grief, therefore, causes feelings that are at odds to the grace and promises of the gospel, and these feelings in and of themselves interfere with faith.

4. Excessive sorrow interferes with hope even more than with faith. This happens when those who consider themselves believers perceive God's Word and promises to be true and applicable *to everyone but themselves*. Hope is that grace by which one not only believes the claims of the gospel but also rests in the comfort that those same gospel promises will be his own specifically, and not just generally. It is an act of application. The first action of faith is to acknowledge that the gospel is true and promises grace and future glory through Christ. The second action is when that faith says, as it were, "I will trust *my* soul and *my* all upon that gospel and take Christ to be *my* Savior and *my* help." Hope then looks with anticipation to that salvation from him. Melancholy, excessive sorrow, and dismay, however, quench such hope, as water quenches fire or ice heat. Despair is the essence of such opposition to hope. The depressed desperately would hope for themselves but find themselves unable to do so. Their thoughts about such matters are filled with suspicion and misgivings, and so they see a future of danger and misery, and feel helpless. In the absence of hope—which we are assured is the very anchor of the soul—it is no wonder that these are continually tossed about by the storms of life.

5. Such an exaggerated sense of grief consumes any comfort one might otherwise find in the goodness and love of God, and interferes with love toward God. Such interference is an enemy to living a holy life. It is nearly impossible for someone so troubled to grasp the general goodness of God at all, and even more so to experience him as good and friendly in a personal and intimate sense. Such a soul finds himself, as it were, like a man in a Saharan desert, blistered by the intense sun, about to die from dehydration and exhaustion. While he can admit that the sun is the source of life on earth and a general blessing to mankind, he is only aware of it bringing him misery and death. Those overwhelmed with sorrow and guilt will admit to God's goodness toward others but experience him as an enemy set upon their destruction. They think God hates them, has forsaken them, is resolved to finally reject them, has made up his mind to do so from before time, and has specifically created them for the express purpose of damnation. They would find it nearly impossible to love a human who slandered, oppressed, or otherwise wronged them; they find it even more difficult to love a God who, they believe, intends to damn them, and who has cut off all means of their escape.

6. It follows as a matter of course that these disordered sentiments make for a distorted and highly prejudicial view of God's Word, works, mercy, and disciplines. The depressed person hears or reads Scripture as directed against himself personally: every lament and threatened judgment he takes as intended for him. Yet, he excuses himself from all the promises and comforting verses, as if he has been personally excluded from them by name. So he finds God's mercies as so circumscribed as to be no mercy to him at all, as if God showed them only to taunt him and make his sins less excusable, and the pending judgment weightier and his inevitable damnation even

more catastrophic.[4] God sugarcoats poison and hates under the pretense of love, with the intent of giving him a worse place in hell. If God corrects him, he imagines not that he is being directed toward repentance but that he is being tormented by God ahead of time. Again, these discouraged souls use the language of perdition, as did those demons confronted by Christ: "And behold, they cried out, 'What have you to do with us, O Son of God? Have you come here to torment us before the time?'" (Matt. 8:29).

7. It is clear that such thoughts destroy thankfulness. Far from offering sincere thanks, excessively sorrowful persons reproach God for his supposed mercies, as if they were cruelties.

8. This disordered reason is entirely at odds with the joy offered in the Holy Spirit and the associated peace that constitute the kingdom of God. To these miserable individuals, nothing is joyous. To delight in God, his Word, and his ways is the proof and essence of true spirituality. But those who can delight in nothing, whether God or his Word or their duty to him, are like a sick man who eats his meal out of constrained necessity and despite his nausea and loathing.

9. The above demonstrates that the disease we call melancholy—depression—is opposed to the very sense of the gospel. Christ came as Savior to set the captives free, to reconcile us to God, and to bring us "glad tidings" of pardon and unending joy. This same gospel, wherever received, brings great rejoicing, whether proclaimed by angels or men. But under the influence of depression, all that Christ has accomplished, purchased, offered, and guaranteed appears to be of only dubious repute and, even where true, a cause more for sadness than for joy.

---

4. Such a person misappropriates to himself words that have only ever been spoken about Judas: "It would have been better for that man if he had not been born" (Matt. 26:24).

10. This malady is readily exploited by Satan for introducing blasphemous thoughts about God—as if God were evil—and hating and destroying those who long to please him. The design of the Devil is to present God to us as being like the Evil One himself, who is in fact a malicious Enemy who delights to cause hurt. Since men hate the Devil for his spite, would he not encourage them to hate and blaspheme God, were he able to convince them that God is more evil in intent than he, Satan himself? The worship of God through images is odious to the Lord as it seems to reduce him to the creature used to represent him. How much more blasphemous, then, is it for him to be represented like a malicious demon?! Diminutive, base thoughts regarding God's goodness, as well as his greatness, are greatly insulting to God, as it would be to think him no more trustworthy or better than an earthly father or friend. How much worse are the imaginings of those with disordered thoughts? It would be insulting to righteous ministers of the gospel to describe them as Christ described the false prophets: thorns, thistles, and wolves. Would it not be a far worse crime to think even more vile thoughts about God himself?[5]

11. This excessive sorrow makes people incapable of constructive meditation. It confuses their thoughts and leads them into harmful distractions and temptations. The more they ruminate, the more overwhelmed they become. Prayer is corrupted into mere complaining, instead of supplications arising from childlike belief. It makes individuals ill-disposed toward gathering with God's people, and makes them unable to draw comfort

---

5. Tolkien expresses this innate willingness to disparage and despise the good (and Satan's gleeful facilitation of that despising) through the tragic character of Boromir, who, under the influence of evil, falsely accuses his faithful and true companion of treachery: "'Miserable trickster!' he shouted. 'Let me get my hands on you! Now I see your mind'" (J. R. R. Tolkein, *The Fellowship of the Ring* [New York: Houghton Mifflin Harcourt, 2002], bk. 2, chap. 10).

from partaking in the sacrament of Communion. Instead, they fear participating unworthily and hastening and increasing their own damnation. Preaching and counsel are also rendered ineffective in the face of such thoughts; no matter what you say or how convincing it is at the moment, it has either no effect upon them or only a momentary one.

12. This disorder increases the heaviness of every incidental suffering, falling as it does upon one already in agony, who can find no comfort to offset that misery. Indeed, the depressed do not even find comfort in the prospect of death, as that seems to them only the very gate of hell itself. Life is burdensome, but death is terrifying. They are worn out by life but afraid of dying. Thus, this overdone sorrow overwhelms the individual.

## Causes and Remedies

Question: What are the causes and cures of this excessive and misguided sorrow and guilt?

Answer: With many individuals, much of the cause is to be found in physiological disturbances, physical diseases, and general "weakness."[6] The soul is unable to find comfort to any satisfactory degree. Here again it must be emphasized that the more the condition arises unavoidably from unseen physiological processes beyond the choice and control of the individual, the less sinful and less dangerous to the soul is that state, even though it is no less perplexing but may be more so for seeming to have no demonstrable cause.

### Three Particular Diseases

Three diseases in particular appear to cause excessive sorrow.

---

6. This archaic and nonspecific term may have served to cover the ignorance of physicians as to the actual causes of the problem.

1. Some consist in such intense and violent pain as cannot be withstood. As this is not usually of long duration, it will not be addressed at length here.

2. Others involve an innately strong emotional reactivity, and the lack of an ability to moderate that reactivity is deemed causal. Often very elderly persons who are debilitated are apt to display an ill and volatile temper. Children, on the other end of the age spectrum, cannot help crying when hurt. Many adult women (as well as some men) are also easily stirred emotionally, and only with difficulty do they regain composure. They have little self-control in this regard, and though they are God-fearing, have very sound understanding, and are quick-witted, they are almost as powerless against emotions such as anger and grief (but especially fear) as might be imagined of anyone.

Temperamentally, they are predisposed toward an anxious, fearful discontentment. Those who are not actually depressed are nevertheless prone to immaturity of character, with a morbid and impatient manner, so that they are always disconcerted, offended, or frightened by one thing or another. They are like the leaf of an aspen tree, set in motion and quivering with the faintest vicissitudes of life. The wisest and most patient cannot satisfy and set at ease such a person. Rather, they find offense in a single word or glance, or take fright in every sad news story, or startle at every noise. Some are rather like children who cannot stop crying until their every demand is met. As sad as this is for those who must put up with them, it must be understood that it is even sadder for those who suffer directly from these miserable symptoms. To dwell with the sick in recent mourning is less challenging. Yet, unless reason has been totally lost, these cases are not hopeless; nor do they absolve individuals from all personal responsibility.

3. However, when reason is largely lost through actual disease, recovery is rendered more difficult and protracted. When those already prone to volatile emotions and a nervous disposition become seriously depressed, the conjunction of temperament and illness doubles the resulting misery.

### Reviewing the Signs of Severe Depression and Anxiety

I have several times described the general nature of severe depression and anxiety elsewhere but will review them here.

1. A troubled and unquiet mind becomes a chronic and unremitting condition in which individuals see little or nothing but fear and trouble. Everything they hear and do tends to feed into their fears. Dangers seem all around them, so that everything they read and hear robs them of all pleasure. Fretful thoughts keep them awake long into the night, and then they are greeted with nightmares when they do sleep. They take self-righteous offense at the laughter or mirth of others, yet see the worst beggar's plight as better than their own. They can't imagine anyone else being in a situation as bad as theirs, though I see as many as two or three in a week, or even a day, with circumstances so alike that you might think them the same. They take no pleasure in friends, family, home, or anything else. They insist that God has forsaken them, that the day of grace is past, and that there is no more hope. They believe that they can't pray, yet this doesn't stop them from howling and groaning, even while they maintain that God will not hear them. They refuse to believe themselves to possess any sincerity or grace; they say they are unable to repent and cannot believe; and they think that their hearts are hardened. They are afraid of having sinned against the Holy Spirit. In summary, their constant frame of mind is one of fear, turmoil, and near despair.

2. If you do manage to convince them that they manifest some evidences of sincerity, and that their fears are thus groundless and harmless to themselves and dishonorable to God, they cannot disagree but find no comfort, or at least no lasting comfort. If any relief comes, the fear returns the next day. Console them as often as you will—the fears will return as many times, and quickly, because the cause of their fears is in their physical illness, not their theological misunderstandings.

3. Their misery comes from what they cannot help but think. Their thoughts flow from illness. You might as easily try to persuade someone not to shiver with a chill, or not to feel pain when hurt, as try to keep them from thinking the thoughts they do. It is futile to command them to stop what is so far beyond their control, and cruel to fail to recognize how much they have succumbed to illness and become captives to thoughts they would very much be rid of if only they could. As it is, they are tormented—sometimes day and night—by psychotic thoughts they cannot escape.

4. When these symptoms become so well entrenched, such persons report sensing a presence of something beside them, as it were, speaking to them various things, directing them to do this or that. They will report that at one time it says one thing and at another time something different, and will only with great difficulty—if at all—believe the voices to be the product of their own illness and disordered imagination.

5. In these cases, they are unusually prone to believe themselves to be recipients of divine revelations. No matter what enters their minds, they take its arrival as an epiphany. They might say, "This verse of Scripture at this moment came into my mind," and "this verse at that moment came into my mind," when in fact their understanding of them was

distorted, or the application made of them mistaken, or perhaps they took several texts together but applied them toward contradictory conclusions, as if one gave hope but the other took it away.

In a similar vein, some become convinced that God has revealed prophecies of future events to them, until such foretellings are overtaken by events proving them false, to these individuals' embarrassment.

Some turn toward clear errors in religious matters—that is, heresy—and believe that God endorses such beliefs; and they become solidly convinced of such errors. Indeed, some who were once chronically anxious have been observed to gain peace and joy by such changes of belief, which reinforces their conviction that they must certainly now be in God's way and that their former lack of peace can be taken as evidence of having been in error. Of these, I have known many persons who derived comfort from positions completely contrary to those they had long held. Some have moved so far from the formalists (papists) and superstitious that they have become Anabaptists, antinomians, Arminians, perfectionists, or Quakers; and some have turned from all forms of Christianity to infidelity and, denying any afterlife, have lived in licentious promiscuity. These heretics and apostates do, though, by their actions escape their sadness, so are not the sort of individuals to whom I now address my comments.

6. However, those who are sadder and—paradoxically—better for it, upon sensing this stirring noise within them are often confident of being possessed by the Devil, or at least of being under an evil spell, of which I will say more later.

7. Of these latter, most are aggressively pursued by the intrusion of blasphemous thoughts, at which they actually tremble, though they cannot keep them from entering their minds. They

are tempted and obsessed with doubts about Scripture, Christianity, and the life to come, or to think ill of God himself. At other times they are filled with urges to utter blasphemies against God, to renounce him, and while they quake at the very thought of such a deed, it haunts them constantly; and some actually yield to the thoughts and speak them out loud. Having done so, they hear an inner voice saying in effect, "Now your damnation is sealed. You have sinned against the Holy Spirit. There is no hope!"

8. When things have continued in this manner, in desperation some have made vows never to speak again, or never to eat, and some have in fact starved themselves to death.

9. In a state of desperation and near death, many have reported apparitions of various persons, but especially of indistinct lights during the night around their beds. They are at times confident of hearing voices or feeling someone touching them or causing them injury.

10. They flee the company of others and cannot tolerate anything but sitting alone and brooding darkly.

11. They neglect their jobs and cannot be engaged to attend to their clear and evident duties with any consistency.

12. When their condition comes to its final extreme, they become weary of life itself and are strongly tempted to kill themselves. They are, as it were, pursued by strong urges to drown themselves, cut their own throats, hang themselves, or jump from a great height. To great sorrow, many have done exactly these things.

13. If they do escape such a horrible fate, they are nevertheless left in a miserable and incompetent state.

So, you can see what are the painful symptoms and effects of serious depression, and thus how important it is to prevent it or to be cured from it as soon as possible, long before it

progresses to the end stage as outlined above. At this juncture
it is necessary that I answer a question often asked, namely: are
such symptoms manifestations of demonic possession or not?
And how much of the above can be attributed to Satan?

## The Question of Demonic Possession

To the depressed person who sincerely wants to know, I must
say that an accurate estimate of the Devil's agency may actually
be more comforting than disturbing.

First of all, we must define what is meant by demonic possession, either of body or of soul. It is not merely the local
presence of Satan or his minions or their abode in a man that
represents possession. We actually know little of the degree
to which he is present with a bad man as opposed to a good
one. What is relevant is the degree to which he exercises his
power over someone through effective operational means. For
example, the Spirit of God is present with even the worst
of men and exerts influences toward good in the soul of the
impenitent; but he is a resident and powerful influence in the
soul of a devoted believer, and is rightly said to dwell in the
latter, to "possess" such in terms of ownership through devotion and love. So too, Satan makes all too frequent motions
to God's faithful, but exercises "ownership," as it were, only
in the souls of those whose habits are given over to unbelief
and sensuality.

Similarly, the Devil is permitted by God to inflict perse-
cutions, sufferings, and ordinary diseases on the righteous
through no fault of their own. He is also God's executor of
extraordinary sufferings, especially affecting the brain, in de-
priving people of sense and understanding, working in addition to the purely physiological basis of the disease. This can
be called possession.

As most evil influences on the soul have Satan as their father but our own hearts as their mothers, so it is useful to conceive of most or at least many physical illnesses as coming from Satan, in that they are permitted by God (as in Job's case), though illnesses also have causes directly within the body itself. Although our own faults and predispositions, the seasons, the weather, and accidents may all be causes in illnesses, Satan may nevertheless be operating behind all of these.

When Satan's operation is so direct that we refer to it as a possession, he may still work by means of bodily weaknesses, though sometimes he has been known to work quite above the power of any disease itself, as when those untaught in strange languages speak them unbidden, and those who are evidently under some enchantment vomit what is clearly iron or glass or other foreign substance. On the other hand, he sometimes is content to work merely through the illness itself, as in the epilepsies and psychoses.

### Reviewing Spiritual Causes and Confounds

From this complicated state of affairs, the following should at least be clear.

1. If Satan possesses the body, that is no sure sign that grace is absent, nor will such a possession condemn the soul if the soul itself is not possessed. No, few of God's children are not, at times, afflicted by Satan as God's means of correcting them and sometimes trying them, as was the case of Job. Whatever some may say to the contrary, Paul's thorn in the flesh, described as Satan's messenger to afflict him, seems to have been some specific *physical* ailment, such as a kidney stone, from which permanent relief was not provided, even though prayed for three times. Paul was instead promised sufficient grace to endure what must have been a very difficult ordeal.

2. Satan's possession of an ungodly soul is a miserable situation and far, far worse than his possession of just the body. Nevertheless, not every evil inclination or sin should be taken to represent such a possession, because no one is perfect and free of sin.

3. No particular sin proves Satan's lasting and damning ownership of a person, except that sin which is loved more than hated, and which one would rather cling to than be rid of, and even that, willfully and not reluctantly.

4. This should be of considerable comfort to depressed but honest souls if they have the understanding to receive it: of all people, none have so little love for their sins as those who groan under the burdensome weight of them. Let me ask you: do you cherish your unbelief, your fears, your distracted thoughts, your temptations to blasphemy? Would you rather be rid of them or cling to them? The proud, the ambitious, the sexually immoral, the drunkard, the gambler, the idle gossiper, the grossly self-indulgent: these all love their sins and would not and will not leave them. Like Esau, who sold his birthright for a bite of food, they will risk the loss of God, of Christ, of their souls and heaven sooner than leave a pigsty of sin. But is this your case at all? Do you enjoy your state? No, you are so sick and tired of it, weary and heavy laden, that you are literally called to come to Christ for comfort (Matt. 11:28–29).

5. It is, as it were, standard operating procedure for the Devil to harass, with vexing and unwelcome temptations, those whom he cannot overcome with attractive and damning ones. As he raises storms of persecution against them externally once they manage to escape from his deceitful traps, in the same manner he assaults then from within, to the degree that God allows him.

### Evidence of Satan's Involvement

We do not deny that Satan has been given latitude in the lives of such depressed persons.

1. His temptations are sometimes the proximate cause of the sin for which the individual is corrected by God.

2. His working is often evident in a physiological imbalance in the body.

3. As a Tempter, he is the primary cause of the sinful and vexing thoughts, doubts, fears, and emotional turmoil of which depression can be considered a secondary cause. The Devil can do with us not whatever he pleases but only what we allow him to. He cannot break down our doors, so to speak, but will be free to enter if we leave them open. He can, thus, find it easy to tempt an out-of-shape, obese individual to sloth; an undisciplined and hot-tempered person to rage; a healthy and "warm-blooded" individual to lust; one given to over indulgence to gluttony, drunkenness, or both; and the bored young to wasteful frittering of time with gaming or just hanging out. On the other hand, some individuals, owing to temperament and no credit to themselves, are simply not tempted in these matters.[7] But if the enemy can throw you into depression, he will find it easy to tempt you to be overwrought and fearful, to have distracting doubts and thoughts, to complain against God, and to despair. From there it is a short journey to believing you are undone and to having blasphemous thoughts about God. Or, at the other extreme, it sometimes happens that individuals imagine they have become exalted recipients of gifts of revelation and prophesy.[8]

4. But I hasten to add that God will impute the Devil's temptations not to you but to the Devil, no matter how hideous,

---

7. C. S. Lewis noted in the preface to *Mere Christianity* that he had never once been tempted by some particular sins, and thus he took no credit for having escaped that to which he was never inclined ([New York: Macmillan, 1960], 9).

8. Both extremes are observed, and both are equally erroneous.

so long as you reject them and hate them. Similarly, you will not be held responsible for those unavoidable ill effects of a physical illness, no more than God would condemn a man for raving thoughts or words said in a delirium or frank psychosis. Nevertheless, to the degree that you retain your reason and a will that can govern your emotions, you are to use your reason and will as you can. It is your fault if you do not, though the conditions that make doing so difficult certainly make the failure less blameworthy.

## *Mundane and Usual Causes of Depression*

But it is typical that other causes give rise to the disease of melancholy (except in individuals prone to it). Accordingly, before I address the cure of it, I will speak more of its causes.

Among the most common causes are sinful impatience, discontent, and worry, deriving from an undue devotion to some temporal interest and from a failure to submit to the will of God, to trust in him, and to take heaven seriously as a satisfying reward.

It is necessary to employ many words to convey the truly complicated nature of this disease of souls. The names chosen will hint that it represents the confluence of many sins, which taken individually are no small cancers. Were they the predominant bent and habit of heart and life, they would be signs of a graceless state. Yet, because these sins are hated and do not outweigh grace, and our heavenly portion is more valued and intentionally chosen than earthly prosperity, we can believe that the mercy of God, through Christ, will pardon those sins and deliver us at last from all of them. Nevertheless, it is fitting for even a pardoned sinner to remain aware of the greatness of his sin so that he may be neither partial to it nor ungrateful for the gift of forgiveness.

I will explicitly discuss the aspects of this sin that cause many to be brought into a dismal depression.

It is taken as a given that God proves his servants through various sufferings in this life, and that Christ wants us to bear the cross and follow him with submissive patience. Some are tried through painful illnesses, some by mistreatment at the hands of enemies, some through the unkindness of friends, and some by difficult, provocative relatives and neighbors. Others suffer slander, at times with actual persecution, and many endure losses, disappointments, and poverty.

### Tendencies of the Flesh

1. Impatience is often the seed of the sinful condition. By nature, we are all too prone to look after the flesh and thus too weak in bearing heavy burdens. Poverty adds to those trials a weight that comfortably wealthy persons do not experience; nor are they likely to pity those who do. Two situations are particularly aggravating.

a. The one is when men are responsible not only for themselves but also for their wives and children.

b. The other is when they are in debt. This is a heavy burden to the unsophisticated borrower, though unscrupulous creditors act as if it were a small matter. When faced with such constraints and trials, men are apt to be all too aware of the burden and impatient under it. When they see that their families lack food, clothing, heat, and other necessities, and do not see clearly how to supply them, and when landlords and other creditors are hounding them to pay debts that they simply cannot service, it is difficult not to lose heart and hard indeed to bear with an obedient submissiveness to God. This may be particularly difficult for women and others liable to strong emotions.

2. This impatience turns into a fixed discontentment and restless spirit, which affects the body itself and weighs all the day long as a burden or an uninterrupted gnawing at the heart.

3. Impatience and discontent torment one's thoughts with grief and continual worries. Those so affected can think of little else, and these worries devour the soul and are to the mind like a consuming fever to the body.

4. The hidden beginning or cause of all this is the greater part of the sin, which is excessive love of the body and of this world. If we did not love something to excess, it would have no power to torment us. If we were not so preoccupied with comfort and health, we would find pain and sickness less difficult to bear. If our love for children and friends were not so greatly disproportionate, their death would not overwhelm us with inordinate sorrow. Likewise, if we did not overemphasize physical well-being and worldly wealth and prosperity, it might be easier to endure hard circumstances, difficult work, and deprivation, not only of luxuries and conveniences but also of those things necessary to health or even life itself, if God so wills it. Avoiding excessive love for these things should at least help us to avoid irritations, discontent, worries, and an inordinate sense of grief and loss of peace.

5. There is always additional sin deep in all of us that demonstrates that our wills remain too self-centered and not yet properly submitted to God's will. We really would rather be our own gods, do as we choose, and have what we desire. We lack a proper resignation of ourselves and our cares to God, and rather than trusting like children and being entirely dependent on him for our daily bread, we are instead more conscious of a need to cling to our sense of independence.

6. This attitude demonstrates that we have not been adequately humbled for our sin. Otherwise, we would be grateful

for even the lowest situation, and recognize it to be better than what we actually deserve.

7. Evidently, discontent and worrisome care reflect a great deal of distrust and disbelief toward God. Were we able to trust God as much as we trust ourselves or a faithful friend, or a child his father, how settled would our minds become in the awareness of his wisdom, all-sufficiency, and love!

8. This unbelief has consequences worse than temporal difficulties. It demonstrates that people do not really accept the love of God and the glory of heaven as sufficient. Unless they get what they want or would have for their bodies while in this world, and be free from poverty and burdens, irritations, injuries, and pain—then what a mess! For then everything that God has promised to them both now and hereafter will prove inadequate. When God, Christ, and heaven are insufficient to calm one's mind, then one is in desperate poverty of faith, hope, and love, which are of more import than food and clothing.

### Dark and Deliberate Sin

An additional cause of such a troubled mind is the real guilt of some large and deliberate sin. Conscience is convicted, yet the soul is not converted. Sin is both loved and feared; God's anger terrifies, yet not so much that the deliberately sinful overcome their sin. Some continue in secret fraud and embezzlement, many in drunkenness or pornography of one form or another and its attendant vices, as well as overt sexual immorality. Even though they realize that "on account of these the wrath of God is coming upon the sons of disobedience,"[9] the fury of appetite and lust prevails so that they then despair and sin. Though the sparks of hell are falling on their consciences, this changes neither their hearts nor their lives. There is more hope for the

---

9. Col. 3:6, with marginal reading.

recovery of these than dead-hearted or unbelieving sinners, who carry out their base behavior with a kind of greed beyond remorse and are so blind as to defend their misdeeds and to make a case against obeying God. Brutishness is not as bad as is a devilish malignity. However, these are not the people of whom I speak in my text. Their sorrow is not excessive but too little, so long as it cannot restrain them from their sin.

Yet, if God converts these same persons, the sins in which they now (happily) live may subsequently, upon later reflection, plunge their souls into such deep sorrow so as to overwhelm them. Similarly, when those who are truly converted dabble with the lure of sin and renew the wounds of their consciences through their lapses, it is no wonder when their sorrow and fears return. Dark sins have laid fast hold onto the consciences of many and have cast them into intractable and agitated depression.

### *The Role of Ignorance and Error*

But among those who do fear God, yet another cause of depression and excessive sorrow is seen: ignorance and errors in matters essential to their peace and comfort. I will give details about a few.

1. One mistake is an ignorance regarding the very tenor of the gospel, or covenant of grace, as libertines (sometimes referred to as antinomians) represent it. These dangerously assure people that Christ has done their repenting and believing *for them*, and that they must no more question their own faith and repentance than they would call into question the righteousness of Christ. Accordingly, many genuine Christians fail to understand that the gospel brings unspeakable joy to all who will believe it, and that Christ and life are offered freely to any who will receive him. Furthermore, no sins—however

great or numerous—are excluded from pardon to one who without pretense or reserve will receive forgiveness. All who wish to drink of the water of life may do so, and all who are weary and thirsty are invited to come to Christ for comfort and rest.

But some seem unable to grasp the terms of forgiveness, which are but to consent to the pardoning, saving covenant of baptism.

2. Many of these are also mistaken regarding what use to make of sorrow for sin, and about the nature of hardness of heart. They think that if their sorrow is not so impassioned as to result in tears and to greatly trouble them, they must not be capable of pardon. Even though they consent to the covenant of pardon, they don't realize that God prizes not the sorrow for sin itself but the destruction of pride. A sense of sin, danger, and misery sufficient to engender a humility that makes one aware of the need for Christ and mercy and brings one to sincerely consent to be his disciple is what God requires of anyone to be saved on his own terms, expressed in his covenant. Sorrow need not be quantified meticulously: if it is sufficient to bring about the humility described, such a sinner will be saved.

And as to the duration of godly sorrow, some are of the opinion that the pangs of the new birth must be protracted. Yet, as we read in Scripture, penitent sinners received the gospel quickly and joyfully[10] as the gift of Christ and pardon and everlasting life. Yes, humility and disgust with sin must continue and increase, but our first great remorse over it may well be subsumed by a holy gratitude and joy.

Regarding hardness of heart: Scripture uses this to describe a stiff, rebellious obstinacy that will not part from sins in

---

10. As Paul said to King Agrippa regarding the time it might take to come to faith, "whether short or long," the important thing is that one eventually believes (Acts 26:29).

obedience to any of God's commands or threats. It is often called an iron sinew or a stiff neck but is never used to describe the mere lack of tears or of passionate sorrow in one who is willing to obey. Rather, the hard-hearted are the unrepentant. Sorrow, even for sin, may be excessive, and an emotional person may easily grieve and weep for the sin he or she will not forsake. On the other hand, obedience cannot be excessive.

3. A great many souls are discouraged by a lack of self-knowledge, being unaware of the sincerity God has given them. In this life, grace is weak even in the best of us, and a small amount of fragile grace is not very easily perceived. Such grace is weak and unsteady in action, and is evident only by its actions. Similarly, weak grace is invariably found to reside alongside a too-powerful proclivity to sin. Any sin in heart and action is at odds with grace and obscures it. Such persons possess too little knowledge and find themselves strangers at home, so to speak, and inept in examining and watching their own hearts and holding themselves accountable. So how could any of them, under such obstacles, maintain any solid assurance of their own sincerity? If, with great effort, they acquire some assurance, the subsequent neglect of duty or lack of warmth in it or yielding to temptation or even inconstancy in efforts at close obedience[11] will at once cause them to question everything and decry all their efforts as simple hypocrisy. A sad and despondent frame of mind is always ready to conclude the worst and can hardly be brought to see any good that might be comforting.

4. In such a case, very few are able to derive comfort from mere arid probabilities. As it is, they have no sense of assur-

---

11. "Close obedience" is most readily pictured in a thoroughly and perfectly attentive servant, who does not fail to obey instantly, slacken in attention when awaiting further instruction, or become presumptively forward in doing what has not been required and is not wanted. The lack of further instruction is perceived as its own instruction: to wait. Previously issued "standing" commands are remembered and executed without the need for daily repetition. There is no running ahead and no falling behind.

ance from the offers of grace and salvation, even though they are eager to receive those offers. If no one could obtain any comfort except those who have full assurance of their sincerity and salvation, then despair would engulf the souls of most true believers!

5. An ignorance of the faults of "successful" Christians increases fears and grief on the part of others. They think that because of our preaching or writing we are much better persons than we are. They then imagine themselves to be without grace because they fall short of our supposed virtues. However, if they lived near us and saw our failings, or knew us as well as we know ourselves, or could read all our sinful thoughts and know our vicious dispositions, they would be free of this error!

6. Unskilled teachers (of Scripture) cause grief and perplexity for many. Some are unable to explain to their listeners the tenor of the covenant of grace. Others are themselves unacquainted with any spiritual, heavenly comfort. Some are lacking in personal holiness or renewal by the Holy Spirit, and do not know the meaning of sincerity. They cannot tell the difference between a godly person and an unrepentant sinner. Being wicked deceivers themselves, they blur the distinction between good and bad, and may even take the best for the worst. Others, again, unskilled in matters spiritual, put inordinate emphasis on things that are not even duties, as the Roman Catholics do in their many inventions and superstitions, and as do many sects through their unsound opinions.

Some coarsely and inaccurately describe the state of grace and purport to say with precision how far a hypocrite may appear to walk in the faith without being actually converted, and in so doing discourage and confuse weaker Christians. Those teachers cannot correct the errors of their publications,[12] nor of

---

12. It's probably impolitic to mention any contemporary names.

their own mentors. Some cause men's peace, if not their actual salvation, to depend on controversies beyond their own understanding, and boldly denounce as heretical and anathema matters they do not comprehend.[13] Even the Christian world itself has long been divided into factions by unwise quarrels over texts and competing interpretations. Is it any wonder that present-day hearers of such controversies find themselves confused?

## The Cure for Excessive Sorrow

Having outlined the causes of excessive sorrow, I will now describe its cure. That cure, however, is more easily described than accomplished. I will begin where I believe the illness begins and tell you both what the patient himself must do and what must be done for him by friends and colleagues.

1. First, do not estimate the sin associated with your condition to be either greater or lesser than it in fact is.

a. Too many people believe that their sufferings and sorrows entitle them to receive only pity. They thus take little notice of any sin that may have brought on those sufferings or that they even continue to commit. Unsophisticated friends and pastors may offer only comfort, when in fact a discovery and rebuke of their sin would be the better part of curing them. If they were more aware of how sinful is their overvaluing the world, failing to trust God, having bitter thoughts of him and meager, unholy thoughts about his goodness, and devaluing the glory of heaven (which should give them some solace even in the most desperate state), as well as their being frequently impatient, worrying, and discontent, and their denying previously received mercy or grace, this would do them more good than words of comfort. When, instead, they speak like Jonah, "I do well to be angry,"[14]

---

13. Jude 9–10.
14. Jonah 4:9.

and think that their denials of grace and distracting and arguing against God's love and mercy are their duties, then it is time to let them know how great sinners they are.

b. On the other hand, if they foolishly imagine that all these sins prove them to be devoid of grace and that God will count the Devil's temptations as their personal sins, condemn them for the very things they abhor, and reckon their very illness of depression to them as a crime, these notions need to be refuted and discarded. Otherwise, they might mistakenly relish their disordered emotions and sufferings.

2. It is particularly important not to give in to a habit of an obstinate impatience. Though it is a selfish love—and while sins against God and his glory are worse—impatience must not masquerade as innocence. Did you not count on suffering and bearing the cross when you first gave yourselves to Christ? And do you now think it strange?[15] Anticipate and prepare daily for any trial that God may bring your way. Then you will not be surprised and overwhelmed. Prepare for the loss of children and friends, for the loss of worldly goods, and for poverty and want; prepare for slanders, accidents, or toxins, along with illness, pain, and death. It is being unprepared that makes it seem so unbearable.

Remember that it is but a degenerating body that suffers, one that you have always known would die and return to dust. No matter who is the means by which you suffer, it is God who tries you by way of them. So when you think you are unhappy with only people, you are not innocent of murmuring against God. Otherwise, his overruling influence would persuade you to patient submission.

---

15. The apostle says in 1 Pet. 4:12, "Beloved, do not be surprised at the fiery trial when it comes upon you to test you, as though something strange were happening to you."

Make it a point of conscience to avoid an entrenched discontentment. Don't you have better than you deserve? Have you forgotten how many years you have enjoyed an unmerited mercy? Discontent is an ongoing resistance to God's disposing will, and even a degree of rebellion against it, in which your own will rises up against that of God. It is atheism in practice to think your sufferings are not part of his providence. Do you dare to complain against God and then continue in that complaining? To whom else does it fall to determine your circumstances, as well as the whole world's?[16]

And when you do experience desperation to be delivered, remember that this is not trusting God. Attend to your actual duty and obey his command, but leave it to him what shall come your way. Tormenting worry only increases your sufferings; it is a great mercy of God that he forbids this kind of fretting and promises to take care of you.[17] Your Savior himself has largely, if gently, forbidden them[18] and told you how sinful and useless such worries are, and that your Father knows what you need. If he denies it, it is for a just cause, and if it is in order to correct you, that is still for your good. If you submit to him and accept his gift, he will give you much better than he takes from you: Christ and everlasting life.

3. Determine in yourselves more diligently than ever to overcome an inordinate love of the world. It will put your troubles

---

16. Job 12:7–9:

> But ask the beasts, and they will teach you;
>   the birds of the heavens, and they will tell you;
> or the bushes of the earth, and they will teach you;
>   and the fish of the sea will declare to you.
> Who among all these does not know
>   that the hand of the LORD has done this?
> In his hand is the life of every living thing
>   and the breath of all mankind.

17. See 1 Pet. 5:7: "[Cast] all your anxieties on him, because he cares for you."

18. See Matt. 6:25–34.

to a good use if you can, so to speak, follow them up to their origins and learn what you cannot bear to do without and, consequently, what you overvalue. God is very jealous, even in his love, against every idol that is shown too much affection, and with any of that love which belongs to him. If he takes them all away and rips them from our hands and hearts, it is merciful as well as just. I don't say this to those who are troubled only for lack of faith, holiness, and fellowship with God and assurance of salvation. These troubles might bring much comfort if those troubled persons understood correctly their source and their significance. Just as impatient worry beneath temporal trials proves that a man loves the world too much, so impatient fretting about lacking more holiness and communion with God establishes that a man loves holiness and God. The love of something precedes desire and grief over it. Whatever men love, they delight in possessing, mourn to be without, and desire to get. The will is driven by love, and no one is bothered about a lack of something he doesn't want in the first place.

However, the most common precipitant of intense depression is initially some temporal dissatisfaction and worry. Whether longings or trials, the fear of suffering them or a sense of the unfairness and aggravating nature of them, or perhaps falling into disgrace or contempt—any of these can induce a consuming discontent. When one cannot abide being denied what one wants, and when the lack of it has muddied and so biased a person's thinking, the door to spiritual temptations is opened. So, what began as strictly temporal sufferings ends up being all about faith and conscience, or solely about sin and a lack of grace.

Why were you unable to bear with patience the words, the wrongs, the losses, and the crosses that came upon you? Why did you make such a great deal of these physical, transitory matters? Is it not because you loved them too much? Were you not in sincere earnest when you once called them vain and promised to leave them to God's will? Would you ask God to leave you alone in such a great sin as loving the world or giving his due to creatures? If God were to fail to teach you what to love and what to hold lightly, and cure you of so dangerous a condition as a sensuous and earthly attitude, he would fail to sanctify you and make you fit for heaven. Souls do not go to heaven as an arrow shot upward—that is, against their inclinations; rather, as fire tends to rise naturally and earth to fall—like to like—so when holy men die, their souls have a natural inclination upward. It is their love that inclines them: they love God, and heaven, and holy company, and their old godly friends, holy works, and mutual love, and the joyful praises of God. This spirit and love are like a fiery nature that carries them heavenward. Angels carry them not by force but as a bride to her marriage, who is borne the entire way by love.

On the other hand, the souls of wicked men are of a sensual, worldly inclination; and they do not love heavenly things or heavenly company, and there is nothing in them to carry them to God. Rather, they love worldly trash, and sensual, bestial pleasures, even if they cannot actually enjoy them. Just as poor men love the riches they lack, these souls are frustrated by lack of what they love. It is no wonder that wicked souls congregate with devils in the lower spiritual places while on earth, and that the latter, if God permits them, manifest themselves to the former as apparitions. It is no surprise if holy souls are not subject to such descent. Love is the soul's poise and energy, and it carries souls downward or upward accordingly.

So be done with earthly, base love. How long will you live here, and what will earth and worthless things do for you? Insofar as it may advance holiness and heaven, God will not deny something to submissive children. But to love something disproportionately is to turn from God. This is the dangerous malady of souls and the attitude that drags them down from heaven. Had you learned better how to forsake all for Christ and to account everything else but loss and refuse, as did Paul,[19] you could more easily bear the want of something. Have you ever heard of anyone who was discontent and distracted with depression, grief, and care over the lack of rubbish, or of some trinket, shadow, or mere dream? If you will not look at the world otherwise, then God will cause you to look at it otherwise to your sorrow.

4. If you are not satisfied that God alone, Christ alone, heaven alone is enough for you in terms of happiness and contentment, then look into the matter: you may become convinced. Go, review your catechism and the foundations of religion. Then you will learn to store up treasure in heaven and not here on earth. You will know that it is best to be with Christ, and that death—which destroys all the world's glory and levels rich and poor—is but the common door to either heaven or hell. Beyond that door, your conscience will not ask you whether or not you lived in comfort or pain, riches or poverty, but did you live for God or self, for heaven or earth? And what has had the primary place in your hearts and lives? Were there shame in heaven, you would be ashamed there that you whined and complained for lack of any physical pleasure on earth, and that you went to heaven lamenting because your bodies suffered here on earth. Focus more on how to live by faith and hope and on the unseen promise of glory with Christ, and you will endure with patience any sufferings along the way.

5. Learn to understand how large a sin it is to set our own wills and desires in a discontented opposition to the wisdom, will, and providence of God, and to put our wills before his, as if gods to ourselves. Don't you see that a murmuring heart

---
19. Phil. 3:8.

covertly accuses God? All accusation of God contains an element of blasphemy. For the accuser supposes that God is blameworthy; if you would not dare to accuse him out loud, then don't let the yearnings of your hearts accuse him. Be aware of the degree to which religion and holiness consist of bringing this rebellious self-will into complete resignation, submission, and conformity to the will of God. Until you can rest in God's will, you will never have rest.[20]

6. Consider carefully how much of a duty it is to trust God and our blessed Redeemer entirely, with both soul and body, and all we possess. Is not infinite power, wisdom, and goodness to be trusted? Is the Savior, who came from heaven into human form to save sinners by incomprehensible acts of love, not to be trusted with that which he so dearly purchased? Whom else would you trust? Yourselves, or your friends? Who has kept you all of your lives and done for you all that has been done? Who has saved all the souls that are now in heaven? What is our Christianity if not a life of faith? And has your faith been reduced to this: to become obsessed with care and worry if God does not shape his providence to fit your expectations? Seek first his kingdom and righteousness, and he has promised that all other things will be given to you, and that not a hair of your head will perish, for each is, as it were, numbered. A sparrow cannot fall to the ground outside of God's providence, and is he going to be less attentive to those who desire to please him? Believe God and trust him, and your cares and fears and griefs will disappear.

If only you grasped what a mercy and comfort it is that God requires you to trust him! Had he made you no promise, this would be equivalent to one. If he asks you to trust him, you

---

20. Matt. 11:28: "Come to me, all who labor and are heavy laden, and I will give you rest." "Thou hast formed us for Thyself, and our hearts are restless till they find rest in Thee" (Augustine, *Confessions* 1.1.1, in *NPNF*[1], vol. 1).

can be certain that he will not betray your trust. If a faithful friend who is able to assist you asks you to trust *him* for help, you will not imagine that *he* will deceive you. But, sadly, I have had friends who dared to trust *me* with their estates, lives, and souls, were they within my power, and would not be afraid that I would destroy or harm them; yet these same cannot trust the God of infinite goodness with these same things, though he commands them to do so and promises that he will never fail or forsake them.[21] It is the refuge of the soul that gives me quiet in the midst of my fears to know that God, my Father and Redeemer, has commanded me to trust him with my body, my health, my liberty, and my estate; and, when an unseen and dreadful eternity looms, to trust him with my departing soul! Heaven and earth are upheld and maintained by him; shall I distrust him?

You object: He will save only his children.

I answer: True, and all are his children who are truly willing to obey and please him. If you are truly willing to be holy and to obey his commandments and live a godly, righteous, and sober life, then you may boldly rest in his disposing will and rejoice in his rewarding and accepting will, for he will pardon all our weaknesses through the merits and intercession of Christ.

7. If you would not be engulfed by sorrow, then do not swallow the lures of sinful pleasure. Flaring tempers, apathy, and neglect of duties carry their own degrees of guilt. However, sin that is enjoyed is the dangerous and deeply wounding sort. Flee from the attractions of lust, pride, ambition, and covetousness, as well as from overindulgence in alcohol and food. Run from them as you would from guilt, grief, and terror. The more you enjoy sin, the more sorrow is likely to ensue. The more you

---

21. Heb. 13:5: "Be content with what you have, for he has said, 'I will never leave you nor forsake you.'"

realize it to be sin and indulge in it against a conscience that tells you that God is also against it, and yet you continue in it and suppress your conscience, the sharper will be the pangs of conscience afterward, and the louder it will be when it is finally awakened to repentance. When a humbled soul is pardoned by grace and believes he has been pardoned, he will still not easily forgive himself. The memory of willful sin, the tawdry nature of the temptation that overcame us, and the mercies and good motives that we suppressed to indulge it will make us rightly angry with ourselves. Our loathing of our wicked hearts will not make for a facile or speedy reconciliation with ourselves. Indeed, when we recall that we sinned against knowledge and did so even with a sense of God's looking on, and that we offended him, we will have enduring doubts about the sincerity of our own hearts. We will wonder if we do not continue to have such insincere hearts and if we would not, presented with the same temptations, indulge ourselves in the same way as before. So do not expect either peace or joy while you continue in sin that is both deliberate and loved. This thorn must be removed from your hearts before you will have ease from pain, unless God leaves you to an insensitive heart, and Satan gives you a false peace, which would only be a prelude to greater sorrow.

8. However, if your sorrows are *not* the result of the aforementioned sins, but instead arise solely from confusion about spiritual matters, the state of your souls, fear of God's wrath upon forsaken sins, or perhaps doubting your own sincerity and salvation, then the reproofs listed above are not intended for you. Instead, I will outline the proper remedy for you, which is the cure of that ignorance and those errors which are the source of *your* troubles.

Many are confused by religious controversies, and every contending faction is confident and has a great deal to say, all of which may seem true to the ignorant and irrefutable to the listener. Each faction claims to be the only way and threatens damnation to those who do not turn to it. The papists say, "There is no salvation outside of our church," that is, none outside of the subjects of the bishop of Rome. The Greeks condemn them and extol their own church, as does every faction its own viewpoint. Indeed, some will pursue conversion with fire and sword, saying, "Join our church or go to jail." Or they make their church itself a prison by driving into it both the incapable and unwilling.

Among all of these claims, how shall the ignorant decide properly?

Answer: The situation is a sad one, yet not so sad as is the situation with the greatest part of the world, which is quietly dwelling in paganism or infidelity, or not even concerned with religion at all, but rather follows the customs and laws of its own countries so that they do not suffer personally. It is actually evidence of regard toward God and your salvation that you are bothered by religion and carefully seek to know which is the right way. Controversy is better than an indifferent atheism that goes with what is politically acceptable, no matter what that might be. If you toss acorns or corn to pigs, they will fight for it, as will dogs over meat. But neither pigs nor dogs will fight over gold or jewels, but will tread them into the dirt. But throw gold or jewels before people, and they will eagerly grasp them. Lawyers quarrel about the law, and rulers about authority, while others ignore both. Religious people strive about religion, though with an imperfect grasp of it. But if you will follow these straightforward instructions, controversies in religion need not disturb your peace.

## Approaches to Quieting One's Heart

1. Be careful that you are faithful to the light and law of nature, which all mankind is obliged to observe. Had you no

Scripture or Christianity, then nature (that is, the works of God) would tell you that there is a God, and "that he rewards those who seek him."[22] It informs you that God is absolutely perfect in power, knowledge, and goodness, and that man is a reasoning, free agent made by God and is therefore God's own, subject to his will and rule. Nature tells you that a man's actions are not morally neutral, but that there are some things we ought to do and some we ought not to do. It tells us that virtue and vice, moral good and evil do differ greatly, and therefore that a universal law obligates us to the good and forbids the evil; and that this can be nothing less than the law of the universal Governor, who is God. It tells all men that they owe this God their absolute obedience because he is their most wise and absolute Ruler, and that they owe him their greatest love; this is because he is not only the chief benefactor but also perfectly admirable in himself. Nature tells us that he has made all of us members of one worldwide family, and that we owe love and help to each other. It tells us that none of the obedience to God can ever be pointless or to our detriment. It also tells us that we must all die, and that physical pleasures and this fleeting world will soon leave us. There is no more reason to doubt any or all of this than there is to doubt whether man is man. Accept the truth of this much, and it will help greatly with the rest.

2. With respect to God's supernatural revelation, cling to God's Word, the sacred Bible, written by the special inspiration of the Holy Spirit, as the sufficient documentation of it.

Faith is not divine faith if it does not depend upon divine revelation, nor is it divine obedience which is given to anything other than divine government or commandment. Man's word is to be believed only to the degree it deserves, with a

---

22. Heb. 11:6.

human faith; and man's law must be obeyed accordingly to the measure of his authority, with a human obedience. But these are very different from the divine. There is no universal ruler of either the entire world or the church but God; no man is capable of it, nor is any council of men. God's law is found only in nature and the Holy Scripture, and that is the law which provides the only divine rule of our faith or judgment, or of our hearts and lives. While not every part of Scripture is equally clear or necessary, one can be saved who understands fewer than one thousand sentences of it, as everything necessary to salvation is plainly contained within those limits. God's law is perfect for its intended purpose and needs no addition from man. Cling fast to the sufficiency of Scripture, or you will never know what you should cling to. Councils and canons are far more uncertain, and there is no agreement among their advocates as to which are obligatory or which optional; and there is no path by which agreement about these matters may be reached.

3. Nevertheless, do accept the help that men can give in understanding and obeying the Word of God.

Though lawyers do not in and of themselves make law, you do need their assistance to understand and properly use the law. And, although no men have the power to make laws for the church universal, we still must rely on men to teach us to understand how to obey God's law. We are not born with either faith or knowledge, and we know only what we have been taught, apart from what we gain from sense perception and intuition or gather by reasoning from them.

If you ask, "From whom shall we learn?" I answer, "from those who know and have themselves learned. No name, title, relation, or vestments will enable anyone to teach you what he does not himself know.

a. Children must learn from their parents and teachers.

b. Adults must learn from their qualified, faithful pastors and catechists.

c. All Christians must be teachers through loving support of each other.

But teaching and law giving are two different things. To teach another is but to show him that same scientific evidence of truth by which the teacher knows it himself, so that the pupil may understand it as well. To say, though, "You shall believe to be true what I say to be true," and "this is what it means," is not teaching but law giving. To believe such claims is neither to learn or to know, though some trust in teachers is necessary to students.

4. Accept nothing as necessary to the essence of Christianity and salvation that is not recorded in Scripture and has not been deemed necessary by all true Christians in every age and place.

It is not that we must first be assured that a person is a true Christian in order that, thereby, we might know what Christian truth is. Rather, the plain sense of Scripture tells everyone what Christianity is, and that we may know whom to assume to be Christians. But, if any doctrinal matter is new and has emerged since the apostle's writing of the Scriptures, that matter cannot be *essential* to Christianity. Otherwise, Christianity would of necessity be a mutable faith, and not the same now as it once was; the alternative would be that there were no true Christians before the emergence of that new doctrine. If the matter is truly *essential*, then the church was not the church and no one was a Christian if they lacked any essential element of faith or practice.

Here one must be careful of sophistical deceit: whereas it is true that nothing is necessary to salvation but that which all sound Christians have believed, yet not all that good Christians have believed or done is necessary, much less those matters that the worst Christians (if sorely tempted) have held. Though the essence of Christianity has always and everywhere been the same, the opinions of Christians and their mistakes and faults have never been valid components of their faith or practice. Human nature is essentially the same as in Adam, and in all men, but the diseases of nature are another matter altogether. If all men have sin and error, then so do all churches. Their Christianity is from God, but the corruptions and maladies of Christians are not. You must hold to nothing but what the ancient Christians have held as received from God's Word; yet, because they all have some fault and errors, you must not hold to or imitate *all* of those things.

5. Maintain the unity of the Spirit with all true Christians as such, and live in love in the communion of saints.

That is to say, fellowship with those who both believe and practice a holy obedience to the Christian faith and law. "You will recognize them by their fruits."[23] The associations of malicious individuals, who suppress true practical knowledge and godliness, and hate the best men and instead delight in wickedness and viciously persecute those who out of conscience resist the former's usurpations and inventions, are not the communion of saints. Wolves, thorns, and thistles are not the sheep or vines of Christ.

6. Do not prefer an odd or insular sect over the universal consent of the faithful within your circles or communion, at least so far as the judgment of others is applicable.

Though we do not gauge our faith according to the number of its adherents, and although the largest numbers rarely represent the best, and while a few are generally wiser than most and in cases of controversy, the few who are truly knowledgeable

---

23. Matt. 7:20.

are often answerable to the less informed, Christ remains the Head of all true Christians. He is not the Head of an odd sect or small group exclusively. He has commanded them all to live as brothers, in love and in holy communion. In science, the greater number of those forming a consensus are more likely to be correct than those with outlying theories but who are no greater in ability than the majority. In the end, no matter which side you prefer in nonessential matters of faith, you must always be in unity with all true Christians and avoid unnecessary differences with them.

7. Never prefer a doubtful opinion above a certain truth or duty. Do not reduce certainties to uncertainties, but rather endeavor to clarify the uncertain so that it becomes certain. For example, it is certain that you ought to live in love and peace with all true Christians, to do good to all and harm none. Do not let any differences of doubtful significance cause you to violate this rule and thus hate, slander, backbite, and hurt them over matters that are questionable, indifferent, or nonessential. Do not make the presentation of "mint and dill and cumin," or any other sort of tithe or ritual, outweigh love and justice and the other essential and undisputed matters of the law.[24] It is an unhealthy sect or opinion that opposes the nature and common duty of Christianity and humanity.

8. Serve Christ to the fullest capacity that your knowledge and abilities permit, and be faithful to the truth as you know it. Do not practice sins of omission or commission, lest God in his justice confirm your disregard of knowledge by allowing you to believe lies.[25]

9. Remember that everyone in all the world is ignorant and perceives as if looking into a distorting mirror,[26] and

24. Matt. 23:23.
25. See 2 Thess. 2:11–12.
26. 1 Cor. 13:12: "For now we see in a mirror dimly, but then face to face."

partially; accordingly, the very best among us have many errors.[27] No one has a comprehensive and perfect knowledge about even the smallest plant or animal. And, if God puts up with the numerous faults in all of us, we must certainly tolerate the tolerable in each other. It is appropriate that people be humble, teachable, and willing to learn. As we have encountered few more imperfect than those belonging to sects that have asserted sinless perfection, so we perceive as fallible and error-ridden the Roman Catholics, who claim an infallibility. When they assert that you are bound to believe their popes and councils and thereby see an end to controversy, then ask them: May we here and now hope for an end to ignorance, error, and sin? If not, what hope is there to ending all controversies this side of heaven, where ignorance is itself ended? Controversies about the essentials of Christianity were ended with us all when we became true and mature Christians. The remaining ones will be resolved as we grow in knowledge. Divinity is no less mysterious a field than law and medicine and the like, in which are found many controversies.

10. These limitations notwithstanding, don't deny your need for knowledge or assume that you already have enough! Rather, as Christ's scholars, continue to learn more and more until death intervenes. The wisest still know very little and may continue to learn. There is a vast difference in excellence, usefulness, and comfort between those of clear, assimilated knowledge and those with confused and disorganized misunderstanding.

Put into practice the ten principles listed above, and save yourself from perplexity stemming from doubts and controversies raised by those who are pretentious in matters of religion.

---

27. May we not say with confidence that only God himself is perfectly orthodox?

## Truths about God's Grace

However, if your difficulties are not about doctrinal controversies but about your sins, lack of grace, and spiritual state, then pay attention to the subsequent directions, and this will be curative.

1. God's goodness is equal in magnitude to his greatness, even to the power that rules heaven and earth. His attributes are commensurate, and his goodness will do good to capable recipients. He loved us when we were his enemies, and he is essentially love itself.

2. Christ freely became human and paid fully for the sins of the world as he intended, so fully that none shall perish for any insufficiency in his sacrifice and merits.

3. Upon his own merits, Christ has enacted a law—or covenant—of grace, forgiving all sin and freely giving everlasting life to all who will believe and accept it, so that all their sins are continually pardoned by the terms of this covenant.

4. The precondition of our pardon and life is not that we never sin or that by any price we purchase them of God or acquire them by works valued by God or by any payment for his grace. Rather, it is only that we believe him and willingly receive the mercy he freely gives us, according to the nature of that gift: that is, we accept of Christ—for Christ—to justify, sanctify, rule, and save us.

5. God commissioned his ministers to proclaim and offer this covenant of grace to all people, and to earnestly entreat them in his name to accept it and be reconciled to him; no one is excluded.

6. No one who accepts this offer is damned, but only those who refuse it to the last breath.

7. The day of salvation is never over for any sinner; he may still have Christ and pardon if he would. If he does not have pardon through Christ, it is because he would not have it. And this day of

grace is so far from being over that it comes savingly to all who are willing, and this grace is still offered urgently to everyone.

8. The will *is* the person in God's account, and what one would truly be and have, so one is and shall have: consent to the baptismal covenant is true grace and conversion, and all who consent have a right to Christ and life.

9. The number and enormity of former sins are no barrier to the pardon of any penitent, converted sinner: God pardons great and small for such; where sin flourished, graced flourished even more. Much is forgiven so that people may be grateful and love much.

10. Repentance is genuine, even in the absence of tears and passionate sorrow, if one would rather forsake one's sin than keep it and sincerely (though imperfectly) endeavor wholeheartedly to overcome it. No sin shall damn a man if he hates it more than he loves it and would truly rather forsake it than keep it, and demonstrates this by earnest effort.

11. The very best of people have in themselves much evil, and the very worst have some good. But what is preferred and predominates in the will is what distinguishes the godly from the wicked. Whoever in estimation, choice, and life prefers God and heaven and holiness above the world and the pleasure of sin is a truly godly person and shall be saved.

12. The best among us need pardon daily, even for the faults in performance of their holiest duties, and must daily live in reliance on Christ for that pardon.

13. Even regenerate men often sin against knowledge and conscience: they know more than others, and their consciences are more sensitive. They would be blessed indeed if they could be as good as they know they should be, love God as much as they know they should love him, and be free from all of the relics of passion and unbelief, which are sins to their consciences.

14. God will not regard Satan's temptations of us as our sins, but only our failure to resist them. Christ himself was tempted to the most heinous sin: to fall down and worship the Devil himself. God will charge Satan alone with such blasphemous temptations.

15. The thoughts, fears, and troubles that depression, natural weakness, and a disordered mind invariably cause have more to do with physical illness than with sin. Therefore, these are the least of sins, and no more sinful than to be hot and thirsty when in the throes of a fever; they are certainly less than some sins that might have caused it, and not beyond the remaining powers of reason to resist.

16. To be certain of our faith and sincerity is not a prerequisite for salvation, though the sincerity of faith itself is necessary. He shall be saved who gives himself up to Christ, though he is uncertain about the degree of his own sincerity in doing it. Christ knows his own grace, even when those who possess grace may have doubts about it. Few true Christians attain certainty of salvation; weak grace mixed with great corruption is uncommon but is rather associated with fear and doubting.

17. The probability of sincerity and trust in Christ may cause one, quite properly, to live and die in peace and comfort without an actual certainty. Otherwise, few Christians would live and die in peace; yet, we see by experience that many do. The common opinion of most church writers for four hundred years after Christ was that inconsistent Christians might fall from a state of grace, in which, had they persevered, they would have been saved. So it was held that only strong, confirmed Christians, at most, could be sure of salvation. This remains the opinion of many Protestant churches, yet those adherents do not live in despair or terror. No one is certain that he will not fall as terribly as did David and Peter. Though individuals have no reason to think it likely, they need not live in terror

because of the uncertainty. No wife and child are 100 percent certain that their husband and father will not murder them, and yet they may live peacefully without fear of such an outcome.

18. Faith may be so weak as to be assailed by doubts over whether the gospel is even true and whether there is even an afterlife; and our trust in Christ may not be strong enough to drive away those fears and worries. Yet, if we hold the gospel to be credible and a better life after death to be probable to the degree that we fix our hopes and choices on them, resolve in those hopes to seek first God's kingdom and his righteousness, would lose all that the world offers rather than trade those hopes, and live a holy life so as to obtain them, then this kind of faith will save us.

19. But God's love and promise in Christ are so sure a basis for faith and comfort, it is both a great duty and benefit for everyone to trust him in confidence and quietness, and then to live in the joy of holy trust and hope.

20. If anyone doubts his salvation because of the magnitude of his sins, the quickest route to peace is to be willing now to forsake them. One who complains about the gravity of those sins is either willing to be holy and forsake those sins or not. If you are unwilling to leave them but love them and would continue in them, why do you complain and mourn about what you are so fond of? If your child cried and wailed because his apple was sour, but wouldn't stop eating it, you would not pity but rebuke him as being petulant. But if you are in fact truly willing to depart from a sin, you are already saved from its damning guilt.

21. If you doubt the sincerity of your faith and the other graces, and all your self-examination leaves you still uncertain, the way to end your doubt is by actually giving yourself to Christ. Are you uncertain as to whether you have been until

now a true believer? You may be sure that Christ is offered to you now: consent to the covenant of grace and accept its offer, and you may be sure that he is yours.

22. Self-examination should not be the only way assurance is sought. Strive to stir up and put to active use the grace you wish to be assured that you possess! The way to be sure you believe and love God is to study the promises and goodness of God until active faith assures you that you do love them.

23. We are made certain of the state of our souls not by any single and extraordinary act, good or bad, but by the predominant inclination, direction, and tenor of our hearts and lives.[28]

24. Though we cry out that we cannot believe and cannot love God and are unable to pray properly, Christ can help us. Without his grace we can do nothing, but his grace is sufficient for us, and he does not deny us further help after he has made us willing. Rather, he tells us to ask it of God, who gives to all liberally and doesn't chide for former foolishness, but gives his Spirit to those who ask him.[29]

25. That sin, known as the sin against the Holy Spirit is not the sin of anyone who believes Jesus to be the Christ. Nor is it the sin of those who fear committing it, nor of every unbeliever, but only of a few obstinate and unbelieving enemies. It is only this: when men see such miracles of Christ and his Spirit that should or could convince them that he is of God, and when they have no other contrivances, yet they would rather claim that he is a conjurer and has worked by the power of the Devil.

26. Though sinful fear is very troubling and not to be loved, God often permits it and uses it for good, to keep us from being bold about sin, and from those sinful pleasures and love of the

28. Charles Williams has argued that each step we take is in the direction of either heaven or hell. See, for example, Williams, *Descent into Hell* (Grand Rapids, MI: Eerdmans, 1975).

29. James 1:5.

world, presumption, and security which are far more dangerous. It may be used to humble pride and keep us in an alert,
watchful state of mind. Justified fear is intended to preserve us
from the hurt and danger feared.

27. One who goes in fear and trembling to heaven will, once
there, be quickly beyond all fear, doubt, and heaviness forever.

28. When Christ was in agony for our sins and cried out,
"My God, my God, why have you forsaken me?"[30] he was nevertheless beloved by his Father. He was tempted that he might
comfort those that are tempted, and suffered such derision that
he might be a compassionate High Priest to others.

29. To the degree that the struggles, blasphemous temptations,
doubts, and fears are grievous, distasteful, and hateful to anyone,
to that degree and more may that same person be assured that they
will not condemn, because they are not cherished sins.

30. All our troubles are under God's sovereign rule; it is far
better for us to be subject to his choice and disposition than to
our own or that of our dearest friends. He has promised that
all things will work together for our own good.[31]

31. A deliberate delight in God and goodness, and a joyful,
praising frame of mind stemming from a belief in the love of
God through Christ are far more to be desired than grief and
tears. The latter serve only to wash away some dirt, so that love,
joy, and thankfulness may enter, which represent the true evangelical Christian temper and are most like the heavenly state.

Meditate on and apply these truths, and they should cure you.

### Additional Remedies

However, if depression has already taken hold, then additional
appropriate remedies must be employed. The difficulty is

---

30. Matt. 27:46.
31. Rom. 8:28.

considerable, because the illness itself causes people to be arrogant, unreasonable, obstinate, and undisciplined. They can hardly be convinced that the illness is physical rather than only spiritual, and they believe that they have sound reasons for everything they think and do. Even if they admit to their irrationality, they blame it on disability, saying, "We cannot think and behave any other way."

On the assumption that there remains some degree of reason, I will offer them additional counsel; and what they cannot do, their friends must strengthen them to do, which I will address as well.

1. Reflect that it should be easy for you in your confused and anxious thought to grasp that your understanding is not as sound and strong as that of others. Accordingly, do not be stubborn and arrogant or imagine your thoughts to be more accurate than theirs. Rather, believe wiser people, and be guided by them.

Answer this: Do you know any pastor or friend wiser than you yourself? If you answer no, then you expose your foolish pride! If you answer yes, then ask that pastor or friend what he thinks of your condition, and believe him and be guided by him rather than by your disordered thoughts.

2. Do your troubles do you more good than harm? Do they make you more or less fit to believe and love God, rejoice in him, and praise him? If you sense that they are opposed to all that is good, you may be certain that they are temptations from the Devil and pleasing to *him*. So, will you love or plead for the work of Satan, which you know to be against your own person as well as God?

3. Avoid ruminations and don't think too deeply or too much. Lengthy meditation is a duty for some, but not for you, any more than it is a duty for someone to walk to church with a broken leg or a sprained ankle. Such a person must rest and protect it until it is mended and strong. So, you may live in

faith and fear of God without requiring of yourself deep and disturbing thoughts. Those who cannot or will not accept this counsel must be roused from their ruminations by their friends, who should direct them toward other thoughts.

4. Therefore, spend little time alone but much time in pleasant, cheerful company: solitude only provokes dark thoughts. Similarly, don't engage in lengthy private prayers, but pray more often and out loud in the company of others.[32]

5. Set your thoughts on the things you know to be right and good: don't focus on yourself and your own heart. Even the best may find within much to trouble them. As turning millstones only wear themselves down in the absence of grain to grind, so do the thoughts of the depressed when they think only of the troubles of their own hearts. To the degree that you can, direct your thoughts toward these four matters:

a. the infinite goodness of God, who is more full of love than is the sun of light;

b. the immeasurable love of Christ in redeeming mankind, and the sufficiency of his sacrifice and merits;

c. the free covenant and offer of grace, which give pardon and life to all who neither prefer sin nor obstinately refuse them to the end;

d. the inconceivable glory and joy that all the blessed have with Christ, and that God has promised with his oath and seal to everyone who consents to the covenant of grace and are willing to be saved and ruled by Christ.

These thoughts will alleviate depressive fears.

6. Don't get into a complaining mode, but speak most of the great mercies of God that you have in fact received. Do you

---

32. Baxter here is warning against solitude for those who are depressed, not against solitude or private devotions in principle.

dare to deny them? If not, are they not more worthy of discussion than your present sufferings? Don't tell everyone about your troubles; doing so magnifies them and discourages others. Speak of them only to your closest friends and counselors. If you speak as much as possible of God's love and the riches of grace, this will divert and sweeten even your bitter thoughts.

7. Determine to spend most of your time thanking and praising God, especially when you pray. If you cannot do so with joy as you *should*, then do so as you *are* able. Do you not control your own tongue? Then don't say that you are not fit to offer praise with your mouth unless your heart is full of it and you are certain of being God's child. Everyone—good and bad—is obligated to praise God and to be thankful for all that he or she has received, and to do so as well as possible, rather than leave it undone. Most Christians lack assurance of their adoption; must they then withhold praise and thanksgiving from God? Offering it as you can is the way to be able to do it better. Thanksgiving generates thankfulness in the heart; your objection to offering it may unmask the purpose of the Devil and his use of your depression to achieve it. He would discourage you from being thankful to God, and from even mentioning his love and goodness in your praises.

8. When tormenting or blasphemous thoughts are thrust into your mind by Satan, don't entertain them, and don't be worried too much over them. First use your remaining reason and strength to resolutely dismiss them and turn your thoughts elsewhere. Don't say to yourself, "I just can't." If necessary, find companions or engage in some activity that will divert you. What would you do if you were to encounter a deranged person in public shouting at you or loudly reviling God? Would you stand there and listen? Or argue with someone in that condition? Would you not leave and so avoid hearing or debating with such a person? So, in your case, when Satan feeds your

mind ugly, despairing, or complaining thoughts, turn away from them to other thoughts or activities.[33] If you are unable to do this on your own, speak to a friend when the temptation arises, and it will become the duty of your friend to divert you by other topics or by bringing you into the company of others.

But don't let this temptation bother you too much, for worrying about it will keep the evil matter in your memory and tend to enlarge it, the way a scratched insect bite becomes redder and more irritated. And it is the *purpose* of Satan to give you troubling thoughts, and to compound these by making you worry about *them*. So one troubled thought leads to another, and so on, as waves in the ocean follow each other. Even the best of people are tempted. As already mentioned, *Christ was tempted by idolatry*. When you do have such thoughts, thank God that Satan cannot force you to love them or consent to them.

9. Again, recall the comforting evidence you carry within you that your sin is not damning: you don't love your sin but rather hate it and are weary of it. Few sinners take *less* pleasure in their sins than do the depressed, and it is only beloved sins that undo people.

Take care to avoid idleness and rather be engaged in regular and proper duties, to the degree that you have physical strength to do so. Idleness is always a sin, and labor is one's duty. Idleness serves merely as a platform for Satan's temptations, and for useless, distracted ruminations. Work, on the other hand, is good for both others and ourselves; both body and soul require it. "Six days you shall labor,"[34] and you must not eat the "bread of idleness."[35]

---

33. D. Martyn Lloyd-Jones says, "The main trouble in this whole matter of spiritual depression in a sense is this, that we allow our self to talk to us instead of talking to our self." (Lloyd-Jones, *Spiritual Depression: Its Causes and Its Cure* [Grand Rapids, MI: Eerdmans, 1965], 20). I have in professional practice regularly advised patients to speak to themselves, out loud, the things they know to be good and true, and so at least reduce the volume of the accusations they are so used to hearing.

34. Ex. 20:9, the fourth commandment.

35. Cf. Prov. 31:27.

God has made labor our duty and will bless us through it in his appointed way. I have seen serious depression cured and turned into a life of godly cheerfulness primarily through a consistent and diligent engagement in domestic and workplace duties. Such engagement moves thoughts away from temptations and leaves the Devil without an opportunity. It pleases God if done in obedience, and purifies the disordered humors.[36] Many thousands of working people live in poverty and have wives and children who feel the grip of it; one might expect them to be distracted by cares and sorrows. However, few of them are afflicted by the disease of melancholy, because work keeps the body fit and occupies them so that they have no time for depressive reflections. On the other hand, in London and other large cities, when the idle unemployed fall into poverty, especially through profligate living, they are miserable indeed: continually vexed, distracted by discontent, and restless in mind. So, if you cannot persuade yourself to stay busy, your friends, if they are able, should compel you to do so.

If the Devil, in his pretense of being religious, appears as an angel of light and tells you that this business is turning your thoughts from God, and that worldly thoughts and occupations are unholy and suited only for worldly men, then tell him that Adam in his innocence was to tend and cultivate his garden; and Noah, having all the world before him, was a farmer. Abraham, Isaac, and Jacob tended sheep and cattle, and Paul made tents. Christ himself is rightly considered to have worked at his supposed father's trade, and he went fishing with his disciples. Paul said that idleness is undisciplined living, and "if anyone is not willing to work, let him not eat."[37] God made both soul and body, and has assigned work for both.

---

36. Baxter used the term "distempered blood," by which he probably referenced the prevailing notion that poisons were released into the blood during illnesses, for which one "cure" was bleeding.

37. 2 Thess. 3:10.

If you find yourself alone and out of the hearing of others, I advise this: rather than engaging in lengthy meditation or long prayers, sing a psalm of praise to God, such as Psalm 23 or Psalm 133 or some such. This will revive your spirit to the sort of holy feelings that are acceptable to God and more suitable to the hopes of a believer than are your dejected worries.

## The Roles of Friends and Family

I am not finished listing the duties of those who care for depressed, melancholy persons, particularly responsibilities of husbands to their wives (as it is much more frequently a disease of women than of men). When the disease itself keeps them from helping themselves, then most of their help from God will come through others. This help will be of two types: first through prudent example and then through medicine and diet, and probably some of each.

1. A considerable part of their cure lies in being agreeable in dealing with them, and avoiding disagreeable things to the degree that is proper, though not beyond. A disagreeableness is so intrinsic to the disease itself that a husband with a wife so afflicted is obliged to do his best to cure her through genuine love and the bond uniting them, and for his own peace of mind as well. It is a real failing in men whose wives, because of personality, melancholy, or disturbed reason, will not yield to reason, if these men then vent their own frustration on their wives and thus provoke them further. You did enter marriage for better or worse, for sickness and health. If the person of your own choosing now, like a child, demands everything she cries for and must be spoken to only in pleasing tones as if rocked to sleep, lest she cry more, then you must condescend to do so. Bear the burden you have chosen so that it does not, for you, grow even heavier. Your own anger and petulance toward someone who

cannot cure her own unpleasant deportment is more culpable than hers, as you retain the power of reason, which she has lost.

If you are already aware of something harmless that will bring pleasure, whether in the form of speech, companions, attire, furnishing, or attention, provide it. If you know something that is irritating, then remove it. Now, I'm referring not to those who are so agitated as to require restraint but to those who are sad and melancholy. If you are able to bring them pleasure, you might do them real good.

2. As much as possible, distract such individuals from the thoughts that so preoccupy and torment them. Focus them on other conversation and matters. Intrude into their space and interrupt their ruminations. Rouse them from such musings with loving and unwavering insistence. Don't allow them to spend too much time alone, but arrange for suitable companions to be with them, or take them to visit friends. Be especially careful not to let them be idle, but press or entice them into some pleasant activity that may entail physical as well as mental action. If they are voracious readers, don't let them read for too long a period at once, and see that they avoid material that is likely to be ill-suited to their condition. It may work well for someone else to read aloud to them. The books by Dr. Sibbes,[38] along with light historical novels or general news of recent events, may serve to take their thoughts from themselves.[39]

3. Frequently bring to their attention great truths of the gospel that are likeliest to bring them comfort. Read them instructive and comforting books, and see that your life with them is both loving and cheerful.

4. Ensure that they are under the care of a prudent and capable Christian pastor, both for confidential counsel and for public

---

38. Richard Sibbes (1577–1635) was an early Anglican Puritan and the author of *The Bruised Reed*.
39. It may be more useful in our day to avoid the twenty-four-hour news channels.

preaching. Make sure this minister is skillful in dealing with depressed parishioners, and is himself peaceable and not contentious, error-prone, or fond of eccentric ideas. Rather, chose one judicious in his preaching and prayer over one who emphasizes emotion over content. Let it be noted, however, that passion in extolling the gospel promises of consolation is entirely in order, and the more fervently the better. Direct depressed persons to a pastor whom they already admire and respect and will listen to.

5. Endeavor frequently to convince them what a great slight it is to the God of infinite love and mercy, and to a Savior who has so wonderfully expressed his love, to think worse of God than one would of a friend—or even of a personal enemy—and to remain unconvinced of that love which has been revealed by the most tremendous miracle. If they had a father, husband, or friend who had risked his life for them and given them all his wealth, would it not be a shameful ingratitude and offense to suspect that he still intended ill against them, and plotted harm to them, and did not love them? How might God and our Savior have come to deserve being regarded that way? Although many say that it is not God that they distrust but themselves, they only obscure their misery by this error, while denying God's greatest mercies: though they desperately would have Christ and grace, they will not believe that God who offers them will actually give them, but think he will damn without recourse a poor soul who wants to please him and would rather have his grace than all the sinful pleasures of the world.

6. Take them out to meet new people. Usually, they will respect strangers, and new faces will divert them, especially when traveling outside of familiar places, provided they can withstand the travel.

7. It is also useful if you can engage them in providing comfort to others who are worse off than they. This will convince

them that their own case is not unique, and they will actually be encouraging themselves as they encourage others. In my own personal experience, a primary way to resolve my own doubts about the state of my soul was through frequently comforting others that had the same doubts, and whose lives persuaded me of their sincerity.[40]

Similarly, it might be a useful exercise to connect them with someone who is mistaken about some matter of doctrine about which they themselves are quite clear and articulate. In this way, as they engage their own wits to convince another of his error and refute it, they may find their own thoughts turned from their own distress. Forester[41] reports that a depressed patient of his—a Roman Catholic[42]—was cured when the Reformation came to his country. His cure came through his eager and frequent arguments against it. A better cause might have even better results.

8. If other means fail, do not neglect medication. Although many are averse to it and maintain that their illness is "only" in the mind, they must be persuaded or compelled to take it. I have known of a woman bound deep in melancholy who for the longest time would not speak, take medicine, or permit her husband to leave the room; he died of grief over this, though she herself was cured by medication literally forced upon her.[43]

Were the malady, as some fancy, a manifestation of demonic possession, medication might nevertheless provide deliverance. If you cure the depression, the Evil One's resting place is removed, along with the condition that served to his advantage. Cure the disorder, and the disordered operations of the Devil cease. It is, after all, through means and temperaments that he works.

---

40. Baxter's unusual self-revelation here is in contrast to his more characteristic style of sharing in general terms how others have been helped.

41. Presumably a sixteenth-century predecessor, given the reference to the Reformation.

42. Baxter used the then-common vernacular "papist."

43. In Baxter's original, "put down her throat with a pipe by force."

Do chose a physician who is actually skilled in treating psychiatric disorders and has a good record of curing others. Avoid women,[44] ignorant boasters, and young and inexperienced men, as well as hasty, hurried, heavy-handed, reckless men who do not have or take the time to study and understand the patient's temperament and illness. Rather, select experienced physicians known to be shrewd under pressure.

Medical treatment and spiritual counsel have not traditionally been provided by the same individual; however, in the case of the confluence of medical and spiritual troubles, combined treatment by one skilled in both may be appropriate. If an older, experienced, highly skilled, honest, careful, and astute physician is available, by all means consult him.[45] Please do not take it upon yourself to use any medicines or other remedies except on the advice of your personal physician. This is because there is wide variation between individuals, and because the *causes* of the same symptoms may be very different. What might be a cure for one may be positively harmful for someone else.

Because many who cannot afford a physician or proper medications may seek out unskilled "healers," and because even among available physicians there is a wide variety of experience and expertise, caution is needed. Some empirically and rashly prescribe without first understanding either the body or the disease.[46] Doing so can be harmful or lethal. There *are* agents

---

44. Given the Puritan's high view of women as coequal partners in life and faith, it is likely that Baxter has a specific group in mind, perhaps—this is conjecture—self-taught herbalists or healers.

45. Baxter here, it seems, excuses his own role as a lay physician when Kidderminster had no fully qualified physician of its own. He did eventually recruit one.

46. "Empirical" treatment is, crudely put, using a medicine without a clear sense of what is actually wrong, hoping that it may help and, by doing so, establish a diagnosis of sorts. This is not uncommonly seen today in the prescribing of modern antidepressants, particularly the selective serotonin reuptake inhibitors (SSRIs), which include Prozac (fluoxetine), Zoloft (sertraline), and related agents. The failure of these medications to provide relief is thus, at times, because they are prescribed when the underlying cause requires a very different medication. Alternately, they may effectively mask symptoms of another illness and inadvertently delay definitive treatment.

that I can suggest which are safe and unlikely to cause major side effects, but my recommendation of them would likely bring me censure from qualified physicians. Nevertheless, some of these physicians, when first licensed—though much younger than I—dare to venture much further than would I, and at great financial cost and harm to their patients.

The *formal* cause of depression is to be found in the emotions, which, when disordered, are unable to perform their proper functions of guiding the imagination, understanding, memory, and affections. So, when the regulation of mood is disordered, the ability to think is impaired and becomes like an inflamed eye or a sprained foot, quite unable to serve its proper function.

The underlying problem is usually some sort of thinning or other weakening of the blood, which is considered to be the "vehicle" of the emotions. Usually that in turn is associated with some dysfunction of the stomach, spleen, liver, or other organ, all collectively deemed to be crucial to the building, circulation, and filtering of the blood. The manifestations of diseases in these organs are so multifaceted and diverse that they are difficult to understand even for the most skilled of physicians. The spleen is often blamed, and rightly so, with the stomach, pancreas, mesentery, omentum, liver, and kidneys not uncommonly involved. Sometimes the effect is to obstruct the humors, and in various ways—at times by the formation of stones, but sometimes by collections of fluid. However, obstructed or swollen spleens are suspected most often.[47]

A distinct, black humor called melancholy—blamed from ancient times—is actually rarely observed, unless you so name either blood or excrement that has turned black by necrosis through stasis and lack of stimulation.[48] Yet, the blood itself

47. Baxter's constructs here are somewhat embarrassing to even the twenty-first-century layperson. But he reflects what was in his day commonly accepted medical ideas.
48. Baxter is likely referring to discolored bodily waste products.

may be called melancholic when it has become distempered through corruption and turbidity, increased viscosity, or alteration that disposes it to the effects of melancholy.[49]

Nevertheless, otherwise healthy persons are sometimes suddenly thrown into acute depression by a terrific fright, the death of a friend, some great loss or suffering, or sad news, and that even within the frame of an hour. So depression is shown to occur in the absence of the predisposition of a melancholy temperament or of preceding illness of any sort.

But the action of the mind suddenly disorders the emotions and disturbs the spirits,[50] which in turn weaken the blood; the weakened blood in time weakens the organs it supplies, until the confluence results in a sick soul and a sick body.

It is often very useful if the physician can ascertain where the illness began, whether in the mind or the body, and if the latter, whether in the blood or the vital organs, since the treatment must fit the condition.[51] On the other hand, a depressed mind may find relief, and the mental impairment may be suppressed, even in the presence of an obstructed or fibrotic spleen, though untreated for many years.

When the disease begins in the mind and spirits, and the body is healthy, medicine—even very harsh medicine[52]—may cure the depression, even though patients may protest that

49. The terms related to the humoral theory of medicine to which Baxter refers are difficult to translate and impossible to make sense of.

50. It is not immediately clear what Baxter refers to when he uses the term "spirits." Common modern usage would be found in the phrase "he is in low spirits today," referring not to the singular spirit of a person but to what might have been also termed "humors" in Baxter's day. But the gist of the meaning appears be a form of vital energy that, when weakened, has a cascading and negative impact on the entire body. Such a concept is not inconsistent with Rudolph Steiner's fourfold system of classification of the elements that constitute humankind (physical, etheric, astral, and ego), but does not mirror it, and it would be anachronistic to strain the seeming parallel.

51. I have noted, on occasion, that correcting something as seemingly simple as a deficiency of vitamin D can relieve depression without additional treatment. This is not typical but supports Baxter's contention that curing the body may cure the mind as well.

52. Baxter cites "purging," a particular crude and even dangerous treatment once thought to relieve the body of poisons. While the concept is abhorrent to modern

medicine cannot cure souls. Yet the soul and body are intrinsically and wonderfully partnered in both disease and healing. Though we may not understand the mechanism behind this interaction, experience informs us that it is real, and thus we have a rationale to use medicine for the body to treat the mind.

Diet can be a significant part of a cure, as I have suggested elsewhere. It is important that the patient be indulged to some degree while still being treated as a competent individual and simultaneously kept from solitude and fretful worry, as well as protected from depressing and troubling conversation and situations. Patients' questions about their treatment should be answered carefully, and any mistakes in matters of religion should be corrected with equal care, particularly if individuals need to be directed from false beliefs.[53] They may benefit from exercise, even vigorous exertion.[54]

As to actual diet, it must be as carefully tailored to the individual as medication.[55] Different conditions should be treated differently. In one sort of depression, the individuals are *only* depressed, with misgivings, fearful thoughts, and despair.[56] They sense themselves doomed and engage in solitary rumina-

medicine, the concept has gained current popularity among homeopathic practitioners who regularly speak of toxins and cleansings.

53. Here, Baxter is speaking of those whose reason remains intact, as opposed to those with fixed false beliefs that will not respond to rational argument or efforts to persuade them of their misperceptions.

54. What your grandmother could have told you has recently been confirmed by research: moderate exercise can relive moderate depression.

55. Dr. Burch was fond of saying, "Sick people need sick people's food. I give 'em chicken soup" (from *The Quotations of Chairman George*, informally published by the Tulane University School of Medicine class of 1974). He meant not that diet alone is curative but that a diet proper to one's condition is integral to the effective use of other means of treatment. Baxter does provide extensive dietary suggestions, which are not included in this work as they are not deemed representative of recognizable or common items in the modern pantry or market. In Baxter's day, diet in the treatment of acute illness of all sorts, as well as in the chronic management of others (e.g., gout), played a much larger role than it does today, though it still remains a foundation for proper management of any number of conditions. Restriction of salt or simple carbohydrates (in congestive heart failure and diabetes, respectively) are only two examples of the continuing importance of dietary modifications in modern medicine.

56. This would represent what today is termed "unipolar depression."

tions, and can neither be satisfied nor comforted. They tend to be morose and inactive, speaking little and moving less.

Another sort of melancholy is represented by those who are easily enraged, display pressured and rapid speech, and are overconfident, are boastful, and laugh readily (and often inappropriately) at anything. They may even report visions and exaltations, and display a euphoric affect. Their judgment is impaired; they are approaching madness.[57] These persons require a very different sort of treatment. For such individuals displaying signs of mania, by all means avoid alcohol or stimulants,[58] as these can lead to frank delirium.[59]

Now, the Devil also has a cure for the sad and melancholy other than what I have prescribed. Namely, it is to cast away all belief in the immortality of the soul and the life to come, or at least not to think of those realities Then one may take religion to be a superstitious, useless fantasy, laugh at what Scripture threatens, and instead spend time in bawdy amusements, gambling, and drinking to escape depression. Ironically, honest recreations are in fact very good for depressed persons who engage in them. However, this cure from the Devil is more like a witches' bargain with the Devil: much is promised, but final payment is in shame and utter misery. The end of that brief mirth is incurable sorrow if timely repentance does not remove the cause of it. The

57. Here Baxter gives a good description of what is known as "mania," either euphoric or irritable, or a mixture of both at the same time. Diagnostically, this description encompasses the bipolar-spectrum conditions and the various schizophrenias. It has long been recognized that medication for unipolar depression is often not appropriate for and may worsen the condition of those with these other disorders. The "madness" referred to by Baxter probably represents delirium, a serious complication of mania.

58. This remains sound advice, and those Baxter described as suffering from mania are the very ones likely to indulge in drug use and excessive consumption of alcohol. Alcohol is generally best avoided in *all* forms of depression, in that, while it may afford a coarse, temporary relief from the misery of depression and anxiety, the relief is fleeting and the side effects serious and longer lasting.

59. Baxter proceeds over the course of several pages to supply detailed recipes for various remedies he deems suited to the needs of particular symptom complexes. These recipes, while valuable to students of the history of medicine and pharmacy, are omitted as irrelevant to the modern reader. Those with interest in such matters should refer to the source material.

stronghold of Satan in the hearts of sinners is strong indeed when sinners are at peace. But when they have wiled away time, mercy, and hope, they yet must die, and then there is no remedy. To go merrily to a hell in which they did not believe in spite of all God's callings and warnings will provide no relief to their torment. To depart this world in the guilt of sin, to end life before understanding the purpose of it, and to face God's justice for such reckless contempt of Christ and grace will sadly end all such joy. As it is written, "'There is no peace,' says the LORD, 'for the wicked.'"[60] Yet Christ says to those of his who mourn: "Blessed are those who mourn, for they shall be comforted,"[61] and "You will weep and lament, but the world will rejoice. You will be sorrowful, but your sorrow will turn into joy."[62] King Solomon assured us,

> It is better to go to the house of mourning
> than to go to the house of feasting.[63]

And,

> The heart of the wise is in the house of mourning,
> but the heart of fools is in the house of mirth.[64]

All said, holy faith, hope, and joy are the best medicine of all.

---

60. Isa. 48:22.
61. Matt. 5:4.
62. John 16:20.
63. Eccles. 7:2.
64. Eccles. 7:4.

*Appendix*

# THE DUTY OF
# PHYSICIANS

## Richard Baxter[1]

It is not my intent to give the learned men of this honorable profession any cause to accuse me of interfering with the mysteries of their art. I will only tell them briefly what God and conscience will expect from them.[2]

*Direction 1.* Make certain that your first and main intention is the saving of men's lives and health. Put this before any consideration of profit or personal honor; though these are also important, they are merely secondary concerns in

---

1. This appendix is a revision of my earlier modernization (Greenville, SC: Reformed Academic Press, 2000) of Baxter's original work by the same title in *A Christian Directory*.

2. On the surface, this seems rather overreaching. However, Baxter does not mean to tell physicians how to practice medicine; rather he addresses under what constraints they should practice.

comparison to human lives. If money is your primary purpose, you reflect poorly on your profession, which, as you practice it, cannot bring any higher honor or meaning than your intentions support. It is the end more than the means that ennobles or corrupts men. If profit is your main goal, it will not matter to you if you achieve it by treating men or cattle, or through less exalted means. You may indeed bring very great benefit to those whose lives are saved through your efforts. However, *the benefit to you will be no greater than your ends*. If you seek to honor and please God, to do public good and to save lives, and *this* is really your primary purpose, then you serve God in your profession. Otherwise, your efforts are simply self-serving. Be careful that you don't fool yourself at this point into thinking that the good of others *is* your goal and more important to you than profit merely because you know that it is more noble and *ought to be* your goal. God and the public good are not actually the true motivations of many who speak highly of these motives, even among those who agree that these should be primary. If most people put their own immediate worldly comfort before the good of their very souls, even while speaking dismissively of this world and calling it empty, then how much more easily might you deceive yourselves and place earnings ahead of men's lives, all the while speaking contemptuously of profit!

*Direction 2.* Be ready to help the poor as well as the rich; do not distinguish between them any further than necessary for the general public good.[3] Do not neglect the health or lives of men because they have no money to pay you: many poor people die because of insufficient means, discouraged from going to physicians because they have no money. In such situations, you

---

3. What does Baxter mean? Perhaps that those who can pay full fare, should, so that those who cannot, need not.

must not only help them *gratis* but also prescribe the most cost-effective medicines.[4]

*Direction 3.* In the absence of true necessity, do not practice beyond your areas of competence. In difficult cases persuade your patients to accept referral to more skilled consulting physicians, if any are available, even though this may work against your own financial interests. You should be above envying the greater esteem and practice due to abler men, and avoid all unworthy aspersions or detractions against them. Rather, you should do your best to enable your patients to obtain second opinions whenever the danger to their lives or health requires it. Their lives are of greater value than your gain. So abstruse and conjectural is the practice of medicine that it requires very high accomplishments indeed to be a physician. If these qualifications are not present—(1) natural sound judgment and the ability to apply it intelligently; (2) a great deal of study, reading, and familiarity with the practice of exemplary men; and (3) considerable personal experience to bring all this to maturity—then you have good reason to be very fearful and circumspect in your own practice. Otherwise, you will sacrifice men's lives to your ignorance and overconfidence. One man highly gifted with all these characteristics may do more good than a hundred dabblers. When you are conscious of a lack in any of these qualities, shouldn't good judgment and conscience direct you to arrange for your patients to consult with those more qualified than you? Should people's lives be put at risk in order for you to maintain a certain standard of living? It

---

4. Medication that a patient cannot afford or obtain may indeed be superior to what he can afford; but if affordability keeps one from the superior medication and no alternative is offered, then it is hardly compassion to brag of offering "only the best treatment." Doing so deprives the patient of *all treatment.*

is not entirely certain that ignorant, inexperienced physicians do more good than harm; accordingly, the uneducated in many areas view physicians with contempt.[5]

*Direction 4.* Depend on God for your guidance and success. Earnestly and intensely seek his help and blessing in all your undertakings. Without this all your labor is meaningless. Consider how easy is it for you to overlook one essential detail among dozens related to the causes and treatment of diseases unless God reveals it to you and gives you powerful discernment and unerring powers of observation! And when twenty essential things are noted, a man's life may be lost if you fail to discern one last point. What tremendous need you have of God's help to bring to mind the most appropriate treatments and, much more, for him to bless them when they are given! The experience of your daily practice should confirm this, unless you have already become foolish through disbelief.

*Direction 5.* Be constantly aware of the fragility of life and of man's mortality, and let this motivate you to be more spiritually minded than other men and more careful in preparing for the life to come by remaining detached from the vanities of this world. Someone who is so frequently among the sick and an observer of the dead and dying is completely without excuse if he himself is unprepared for his own sickness or death. If your heart is not softened by practically living in the house of mourning, then your heart is indeed callous and wicked. It is strange that physicians as a lot are sometimes suspected of atheism and that *religio medici* should be synonymous with agnosticism. Surely this idea arose in some more-secular age or country!

5. In a footnote Baxter says, "Overestimating [pastors'] understanding in religion ruins souls and churches. In a similar manner, overestimating [physicians'] competence in medicine costs many their lives. I do not know whether a few able, prudent, and experienced physicians cure more than the rest [combined] kill."

I have often been very thankful to God in observing the contrary. Indeed, there have been many excellent, pious physicians in most countries where the purity of religion has appeared. How much they have promoted the work of reformation (of whom I might name many).[6] In this country and time, I must confess that I have known as many physicians to be Christians as, proportionately, in any other profession, except preachers of the gospel. But no men are more desperately wicked than those who are wicked in spite of godly education and in the face of powerful means that should cause their own improvement. Accordingly, *it is very likely that those physicians who are not truly good are very bad,*[7] because they are bad contrary to so much revelation and so many warnings. It is likely that the aforementioned, censorious proverb (*religio medici*) came about because of some of these characters. Indeed, man's nature is so apt to be desensitized by things that are unusual and to forget the meaning of things that have become routine, that *no men have a greater need to guard their hearts and to fear callousness than those who are continually exposed to the most heartrending examples and warnings.* It is all too easy to grow dull and accustomed to them. Then the danger is that no better means remain to awaken such a dull, hardened heart. On the other hand, those who only infrequently are exposed to such warnings are not so apt to lose the sense and benefit of them. The sight of a sick or dying man usually arrests the attention of those who seldom witness such things. But who are more hardened than soldiers and seamen, who live continually as among the dead? When they have two or three times seen the battlefield

---

6. Baxter names three who are obscure in our age.

7. Sherlock Holmes, speaking of a Dr. Grimesby Roylott, puts it this way: "When a doctor does go wrong he is the first of criminals. He has nerve and he has knowledge" (Sir Arthur Conan Doyle, "The Adventure of the Speckled Band," in *The Adventures of Sherlock Holmes* [London: George Newnes, 1892]).

covered with men's bodies, they usually grow more coldhearted than any others. *This is precisely what physicians are in danger of* and so should most carefully strive to avoid. But certainly an unbelieving or ungodly physician is inexcusably blind. To say, as some do, that they study nature so much that they are carried away from God is like saying they study the work so much that they forget the workman; or they read the book so much that they overlook the content of it; or that they study medicine so much that they forget both the patient and his health. *To look into nature and not see God is to see the creatures and not the light by which we see them*, or to see the trees and houses and not to see the earth that supports them. For God is the creating, conserving, and orchestrating final cause of all things; "for from him and through him and to him are all things";[8] he is all in all. And if they do not know that they are the subjects of this very God and that they themselves have immortal souls, then they are poor students of nature to remain so oblivious to the nature of man. To boast of their accomplishments in other sciences while not knowing what a man is, or what they themselves are, is small credit to their intellects. You who still live as in the sight of death should also live as in the sight of another world and outdo others in spiritual wisdom, holiness, and soberness, even as your spiritual advantages excel through these unique perspectives.

*Direction 6.* Show your compassion and love to men's souls as well as to their bodies. Speak to your patients words that will prepare them for death. You have excellent opportunities if you have the heart to use them. If ever people will hear, it is when they are sick. If ever they will be humbled and serious, it is when the approach of death compels them. They will then patiently

---

8. Rom. 11:36.

hear advice that they would have despised in their health. A few serious words about the danger of being unregenerate, the necessity of holiness, the role of a Savior, and the everlasting state of souls may, for all you know, be used to bring about their conversion and salvation. And it is much more satisfying for you to save a soul than to cure the body. Don't try to excuse yourselves by saying, "That is a pastor's duty." Though it is theirs *ex officio*, it is yours also *ex charitate*. Love obligates everyone, as opportunity arises, to do good to all, and especially the greatest good. And God gives you opportunity by placing such souls in your path. The priest and Levite who passed by the wounded man were more blameworthy for not helping him than those who never went that way and therefore never saw him.[9] Many persons who would never call a pastor *will* call a physician. Many who despise pastors will listen to a physician. As one pays his mortgage holder because he thereby keeps his house, so does one listen to his physician because he thinks his doctor can save his life. Unfortunately, in too many places pastors either neglect such work or are inadequate for it, or else are aloof and distant from the people. So there is great need for your kind help. Remember then, that "whoever brings back a sinner from his wandering will save his soul from death and will cover a multitude of sins."[10] Remember too that you are about to speak to someone who is going into another world and who must be saved now or never! All that ever must be done for his salvation must be done immediately, or it will be too late. Pity human nature and do not harden your hearts against a man in his extreme necessity. Speak a few serious words (if they are necessary) for his conversion, and do so before his soul is beyond your help, in the world from which there is no return.

---

9. See Luke 10:32.
10. James 5:20.

# GENERAL INDEX

Act of Toleration (1689), 19
Act of Uniformity (1662), 20, 32
alcohol, 139, 167
American Psychiatric Association, 46
anger, 27n, 81, 115, 159
antidepressant drugs, 31, 163–64.
  *See also* medication
antinomians, 128–29
anxiety, 10, 59, 115, 154
apostates, 118
Arnold, Matthew, 54n27
asceticism, 75
assurance, 130–31, 135, 156
Augustine, 29

bad dreams, 28
Baxter, Richard
  biblical commitment of, 50–52, 56
  body/soul views of, 41
  life of, 19–23
  list of "Grand Directions," 23–24
  and soul care, 49
bipolar disorder, 10, 31, 47, 59, 65
Bunyan, John, 13, 30
Burch, George E., 38–40, 42–43, 48, 66, 166n55

casuistry, 19
Charles I, 20
Charlton, Margaret, 22
"chemical imbalance," 47
Christian community, 28–29, 88, 113–14, 145–46
Chrysostom, 60n39
Churchill, Winston, 11
church worship, 12, 18
cognitive-behavioral therapy, 53
covenant of grace, 128–29, 131, 148, 155
creativity, 10

death, 106–7, 114
debt, 125–26
delirium, 82, 167
demonic possession, 120–21, 162
demons, 74, 82
depression
  caring for person with, 159–68
  definition of, 9–10, 31, 74–83
  and gospel opposition, 112–13
  increase of, 45–46
  medical treatment for, 162–75
  and salvation, 25, 74, 76
  seeking help for, 154–59
  as sin or unbelief, 13
  *See also* melancholy

Devil, 74, 80–82, 95, 97–98, 154, 156–57, 167–68. *See also* Satan
diet, 166–67
discontentment, 86, 125–27, 134, 158
duty, 19, 26–27, 80, 157–58

elderly, 115
emotional reactivity, 115
emotions, 73, 84, 93, 96, 115–16, 124–25, 133, 164–65
evil, 96, 105, 108, 113, 118, 121–22, 142, 149
exercise, 166–67

faith
    blockage to, 33, 77–78, 109–10
    certainty in, 150–52 (*see also* assurance)
    and dependence on Scripture, 142–45
    in God's providence, 138–39
    and joy, 13
    that is saving, 29, 85
fasting, 108–9
fears, 28, 74, 81–83, 115–17, 140, 152–53
fruits of the Spirit, 11

genetic conditions, 62–65
God
    blasphemous temptations against, 81–82, 113, 118–19, 138
    feeling rejected by, 75–76, 116
    glory of, 26–27, 90
    goodness of, 55, 84, 111, 148, 153, 155
    knowledge of, 147
    love commandments of, 25–26
    mercy of, 108–11, 129–30, 133

    thanksgiving and praise for, 92–93, 98, 112, 156
    will of, 19, 25, 124–27, 134, 137
    wrath of, 83
grace, 28, 30, 75, 85, 91, 107, 116, 148–53
grief, 109–10, 115
guilt, 31, 63, 107–8, 111, 114, 127, 139

Haller, William, 22
heaven, 26, 78, 86, 90, 127, 137, 149
hell, 26, 106
holiness, 23, 93, 106, 131, 149, 174
holistic care, 37, 40
Holy Spirit, 29, 81, 112, 116, 152
human body
    "humors" of, 27, 44, 47, 164–65
    segregation from soul of, 36–37, 41
humility, 60, 63–64, 99n43, 100, 109, 129, 147

idleness, 28, 78, 97, 157–58, 160
idolatry, 135, 157
imagination
    confusion in, 80, 82, 99
    and exaggerating sin, 74–75
integrative medicine, 37
intellect, 25, 74, 76

Jesus
    fellowship with, 25, 146
    finding hope in, 110
    finding satisfaction in, 137–38
    holiness in, 91
    new nature in, 107
    rejoicing in, 28, 30
    righteousness of, 128–29

sacrifice of, 148–49, 153, 155
and sin versus sickness, 59–65
Job, 11, 58n31, 61, 121
judgment, 105, 111, 167–68
justification, 148

Knecht, Glenn C., 65n

law, 142–45
Lewis, C. S., 123n7
Lloyd-Jones, D. Martyn, 157n33
love
    of family, 25–26
    of God, 90, 98, 135–37, 149,
        151–52, 161
    of neighbor, 25–26, 108

mania, 167
marriage, 159–60
medication, 10, 47–48, 100–101,
    162–63, 171
melancholy, 12, 27–28, 73n2,
    83–84, 164
mental faculties, 109–10
mental illness, 56–58
Myers-Briggs, 44

new creation, 29
nightmares, 116

obedience
    to Christian law and faith, 142,
        145
    to God, 18, 98, 130, 158
    and the mind, 25–27
overwork, 10

panic disorder, 31
pastoral care, 12, 160–61
Percy, Walker, 54n25
perfectionism, 99n43
personality profiles, 44–45
physiological disturbances, 114
piety, 18

poverty, 125–27, 170–71
prayer, 80, 86–88, 107–8, 113–14,
    152, 155
predestination, 75–76
pride, 129, 153, 154
private devotions, 87–88, 100,
    154–55
psychiatric disorders
    denial of, 57–58
    medical treatment of, 163,
        169–75
    nature of, 43
    and sin, 60–65
psychotic thoughts, 117
Puritanism, 18–19, 25–27, 41–42,
    46, 49–50

reason, 109, 116, 124
religious controversies, 140–41
repentance, 58, 75–76, 85, 90, 96,
    112, 128–32, 140, 149
Ross, Mark E., 56n29

sadness, 10, 27, 31, 75, 118
salvation, 84–85, 110, 140–41,
    148–51
sanctification, 148
Satan, 85, 89–90, 94, 113,
    120–24, 150. *See also* Devil
schizophrenia, 31, 47, 65
selective serotonin reuptake in-
    hibitors (SSRIs), 163n46
self-control, 115
self-examination, 19, 79, 151–52
self-knowledge, 130
self-torture, 78
serotonin, 47. *See also* selective
    serotonin reuptake inhibitors
Sibbes, Richard, 19–20, 160
sin
    against conscience, 75–77,
        84, 97, 105, 127–28, 135,
        139–40, 149–50

with delight and obstinacy,
    105–6, 127–30
excessive sorrow over, 74–75,
    77, 104, 107–14
freedom from, 31–32, 96, 151
of ignorance and error, 128–32
mercy from, 91–92, 148–49
and physical sickness, 58–65,
    85, 96, 125, 150
as a spiritual disorder, 23
and temptation, 81–82, 85, 95,
    123–24, 140, 150, 153, 157
solitariness, 28, 78, 155
soul care, 174–75

Spira, Francis, 76
spiritual euphoria, 13
Spurgeon, C. H., 11
Stoic moral philosophy, 51–53
suffering, 124–25, 133–34
suicide, 28, 49, 82, 119
superstition, 79, 108

therapy, 12, 31, 53
trauma, 10, 49, 63

vitamin deficiency, 165n51

Williams, Charles, 152n28

# SCRIPTURE INDEX

*Genesis*
3:19 . . . . . . . . . . . . . .97n41
19:14 . . . . . . . . . . . . . .106n3

*Exodus*
20:9 . . . . . . . . . . . . . .97n40, 157n34

*Numbers*
12 . . . . . . . . . . . . . . . .62n48

*1 Kings*
13 . . . . . . . . . . . . . . . .62n48
14 . . . . . . . . . . . . . . . .62n49

*Job*
1:8 . . . . . . . . . . . . . . . .61n47
12:7–9 . . . . . . . . . . . .134n16
28:12 . . . . . . . . . . . . . .49n21

*Psalms*
23 . . . . . . . . . . . . . . . .159
51:3 . . . . . . . . . . . . . .91n28
73 . . . . . . . . . . . . . . . .61n41, 63n51
133 . . . . . . . . . . . . . . .159

*Proverbs*
20:9 . . . . . . . . . . . . . .59n33
31:27 . . . . . . . . . . . . .157n35

*Ecclesiastes*
4:12 . . . . . . . . . . . . . .9n1

7:2 . . . . . . . . . . . . . . . .168n63
7:4 . . . . . . . . . . . . . . . .168n64
7:18 . . . . . . . . . . . . . .61n43

*Isaiah*
48:22 . . . . . . . . . . . . .168n60
57:1–2 . . . . . . . . . . . .61n42

*Lamentations*
1:12 . . . . . . . . . . . . . .76n7

*Ezekiel*
36:26 . . . . . . . . . . . . .29, 29n11

*Jonah*
4:9 . . . . . . . . . . . . . . . .132n14

*Matthew*
5:4 . . . . . . . . . . . . . . . .168n61
6:25–34 . . . . . . . . . . .134n18
7:20 . . . . . . . . . . . . . .145n23
8:29 . . . . . . . . . . . . . .112
9:2 . . . . . . . . . . . . . . . .59n37
9:5 . . . . . . . . . . . . . . . .60nn38–39
10:22 . . . . . . . . . . . . .68n58
11:28 . . . . . . . . . . . . .138n20
11:28–29 . . . . . . . . . .122
13:52 . . . . . . . . . . . . .47, 47n18
22:17 . . . . . . . . . . . . .61n44
23:23 . . . . . . . . . . . . .146n24
24:13 . . . . . . . . . . . . .68n58

26:24.............112n4
27:46.............153n30

*Luke*
10:32.............175n9

*John*
3:3–12 .............29, 29n14
3:16 .............91n30
5:14 .............60n40
5:40 .............91n30
9:2.................59n34, 61n45
9:3.................61n46
16:20.............168n62

*Acts*
26:29.............129n10

*Romans*
3:2.................56n30
3:23 .............59n36
8:28 .............153n31
9:11 .............59n35
11:36.............174n8

*1 Corinthians*
5....................104
11:28–29 .........80n10
13:12.............146n26

*2 Corinthians*
2:7.................32, 103
5:17 .............29, 29n12
8:12 .............87n24
12:7 .............12, 12n6

*Galatians*
5:22–23.............11n5
6:2.................88n25
6:2–5 .............65n55
6:5.................88n25

*Philippians*
3:8.................137n19

*Colossians*
2:18–23...........79n8
3:6.................127n9

*2 Thessalonians*
2:11–12...........146n25
3:10 .............97n42, 158n37

*1 Timothy*
5:24–25...........64n52

*2 Timothy*
3:12 .............63n50

*Hebrews*
4:16 .............66n56
5:1.................55n28
11:6 .............142n22
13:5 .............139n21

*James*
1:5.................152n29
4:7.................94n34
5:20 .............175n10

*1 Peter*
4:12 .............133n15
5:7.................134n17

*2 Peter*
1:10 .............85n21

*1 John*
2:29–3:9 .........29, 29n13
5:10–12...........91n30
5:16–17...........94n35

*Jude*
9–10.............132n13

*Revelation*
22:17.............91n30

.